Compassionate Leadership for School Belonging

Compassionate Leadership for School Belonging

Kathryn Riley

UCLPRESS

First published in 2022 by
UCL Press
University College London
Gower Street
London WC1E 6BT

Available to download free: www.uclpress.co.uk

A CIP catalogue record for this book is available from The British Library.

ISBN: 978-1-78735-958-1 (Hbk)
ISBN: 978-1-78735-957-4 (Pbk)
ISBN: 978-1-78735-956-7 (PDF)
ISBN: 978-1-78735-959-8 (epub)
ISBN: 978-1-78735-960-4 (mobi)
DOI: https://doi.org/10.14324/111.9781787359567

This book is dedicated to Roberto Molina Rivero and to my grandchildren Clara Jane and Miles John

Contents

List of vignettes, figures and tables

Vignettes

Figures

Table

Preface

A sense of belonging is an intensely personal experience and is shaped by what we bring to it, what we encounter and what others expect of us. When we have a sense that we belong, we feel connected and safe. Our confidence grows – and we dare to dream.

This book brings together many of the threads of the evolving tapestry of my personal and professional life which have contributed to my understanding of the importance of school belonging. I have grown to appreciate how my own heritage, as a child of Irish and Jewish diasporas, has enabled me to understand the importance of identity and belonging, and to recognise how particular events and experiences along the way have influenced my thinking about these issues.

Fresh out of university I found myself at Asmara Teaching Training College, where I came to learn how we can view life in such different ways. In my early days as a teacher, I discovered that you could find a world in a London classroom. In 1981, I was living and teaching in South London, and carrying out research for my PhD on race and gender issues. Two events of that year have long stayed with me.

The first was a fire in nearby New Cross which took the lives of 13 young black people, and the second the Brixton Riot: a clash between a predominantly white police force and black youths. I grew to see the interplay between life on the streets and life in the classroom, and how schools' policies and practices can generate a sense of insiders and outsiders. I began to ask: why is it that most young children start school full of enthusiasm, yet many end up frustrated, sad or excluded?

The initial impulse for this book came from a growing sense of anger about the seemingly relentless rise in the number of young people who felt school was not a place for them. The motivation sprang from the recognition that this was not an inevitable state of affairs. Research and development work on place and belonging (in many parts of the world with DanceTioMolina through our programme 'The Art of Possibilities'; see Appendix 3) had taken me to schools across the globe. I found many which are places of belonging, joy, excitement and wonder.

As I began writing the book, the Covid-19 pandemic sent its first breakers across the globe. The onset of the pandemic rattled preconceptions, challenged assumptions and revealed widening socio-economic divisions and growing levels of inequity. I finished the book in August 2021, as the Covid-19 vaccines began to raise hopes for the future. Pundits talked about a return to a new normality. I was not one of these.

The Covid-19 pandemic had spun the world around. However, a crack in the wall of rejection had emerged, revealing a liminal space, a space in which profound transformation could take place. Such moments occur rarely, and when they do, society 'rearranges' itself in a relatively short space of time (Drucker 1994). I began to ask: could we seize this moment, break from the past and define a new normal which is about possibilities? Could we move away from those practices of exclusion and ostracisation which characterise so many school systems? Could we create school systems which were built on the foundations of connectedness and belonging?

This book is my optimistic response to those questions. The script is not a fanciful one – no Hollywood stars here. The arguments put forward are based on solid research evidence from many parts of the world and the examples draw on the professional practice and wisdom of school leaders, teachers and young people.

My work on school belonging has taught me three invaluable lessons. The first is that system approaches which rely on mechanisms of order and control, over-rigid testing regimes and sanction-driven behaviour management are long past their sell-by date. The second is that young people tend to be happier, more confident and perform better academically in schools where they have a sense of connectedness and belonging, and their teachers feel more professionally fulfilled and valued. The final lesson is that compassionate forms of leadership help grow the conditions for school belonging.

Compassionate Leadership for School Belonging re-examines the past; explores contemporary realities; and steps into the future. This is a brave act for us all. We *do not* know what is to come: across the world, in our country or in our neighbourhoods. However, we *do* know the expectations, beliefs, practices and relationships that can help create the conditions for school belonging. Creating schools which are places of belonging – where children and adults are known and seen for who they are – is our gift to future generations.

I hope you enjoy the book and that it contributes to your thinking about what can be done to help this happen.

Foreword

Karen Seashore Louis

I have been following Kathryn Riley's professional journey for several decades and will take on any opportunity to reflect on the importance of her work. Not surprisingly, I responded enthusiastically to the opportunity to preview this book.

Its larger message is that we can no longer treat schools as institutions taxed with a technical task of transmitting knowledge from one generation to the next. Rather, it is time to face the more intractable problem: The technical task cannot be accomplished without attending to community and belonging. From the sense of urgency felt in schools whose enrolments increasingly reflect families displaced by war or social unrest to the more uneasy but compelling evidence that student alienation from formal schooling is increasing everywhere, Professor Riley develops a picture of a system that has too often mislaid its moral centre.

Her response is not to argue for policy or system change, but for action at the school level. What I have seen in the past few years is Professor Riley's deepened commitment to bringing key ideas about place and belonging into collaborative action-research with school leaders. This book represents what she has learned from this intensive work – an expression of hope for the future of schooling along with a compilation of highly usable knowledge. Starting with vignettes and images reflecting children who feel as if they belong in school, she stitches together a new story about how adults can make a difference. This is, however, intermixed with another story, told with historical vignettes and children's artwork, that reflects generational deprivation and the complex feelings of young people about belonging in schools, particularly those that serve children from immigrant and marginalised communities.

Professor Riley's purpose is clear: as in her action-research work with schools, she eschews an off-the-shelf solution to the disengagement of both marginalised and more affluent young people. Readers will not find a 10-step action plan for making a school an inviting and dynamic environment for children's personal, social and intellectual growth. Instead, this book reflects her experience of co-creating ongoing experiments with adults, children and the communities served by schools, and her conviction that each setting is unique, although the underlying principles may not vary greatly. To paraphrase the tired aphorism, she does not give school leaders a fish nor does she teach them how to fish – rather, she sets out critical ideas and tools that they can adapt to their context.

What are the critical principles? First, except under the most pressing circumstances, children must feel that the school is *a psychologically safe space*. Belonging (or lack thereof) is not a new problem. Ever since the advent of obligatory schooling, institutions have developed ways to exclude some children, either temporary or permanently. One of the most evocative images in the book makes clear the devastating effects that being excluded can have on a young person's identity (Figure 0.1). My colleague Joe Murphy has said for years that the first goal of a school leader is to make sure that there is an invisible cord between a caring adult and each child, so that if the child begins to distance themselves, the adult will see the change and figure out how to draw them back in. This book provides examples of that important insight: the sense of connection is a key element of feeling safe.

Figure 0.1 I don't belong here (Riley and Rustique-Forester 2002: 28).

A second principle that is woven throughout the book is the need for adults to be attentive to the *experiences that each student brings with them*. From Abdi, who gratefully acknowledges that physical safety is fundamental to his feeling of belonging, to the families that experience routinised racism, Riley's work points to the need to personalise educational experiences and the treatment of individuals. In the United States there is an increasing backlash against 'no excuses' school policies that ignore the context that may explain 'unacceptable' behaviour, popularised by Jeff Duncan-Andrade (2012) but reflected in the increasing interest in 'trauma-informed pedagogy'. This book goes much further, however, and defines the community as deserving of the same compassion that is offered to individual students for whom it is home. The focus on community enlarges our perspective on how schools become institutions that look for and reinforce the assets and knowledge that the young people bring with them from their lived experience outside of school.

Not surprisingly, the third principle woven throughout the book is the importance of physical place – *a sense of rootedness* that goes beyond positive relationships and comfort inside the school. So many of the images drawn by children seem to include a heavy line separating their views of school and those of the community in which they live. Yet young people are, of course, experiencing both at the same point in their lives. Most of what passes for research on school–community relations is actually about school–parent involvement, with limited attention to the broader community. But we know that, especially for adolescents, their experience of the world is circumscribed both by family and the larger community and the failure to incorporate community into the school's agenda. Professor Riley argues, persuasively, that ignoring place means denying a critical component of individual sense of identity, but also a critical resource for supporting both technical-measurable learning and the equally critical social and emotional development.

As I pored through the examples, both uplifting and difficult, I could not help but think about how the principles of belonging also colour the lives of so many adults, especially educators. A fourth principle that appears throughout, but is emphasised in the last section, is *how leaders and teachers experience belonging inside the school*. Does the headteacher/principal 'manage' the school and its programmes, or do they walk in the door each morning with a sense of belonging? And do the teachers also experience the school as a safe space that values their unique experiences and contributions, that is located in a community where they have meaningful relationships even if they do not live there? I am reminded of Brian Friel's *The Home Place* (2005). While the play is ostensibly about racism and class as English rule begins to erode in Ireland in the late nineteenth century, what struck me was that the owner of the Lodge at Ballyweg kept referring to a place in southern England where he had not lived for decades as his real home. In other words, you can occupy a place for a long time without feeling as if it is where you really belong. Explicit in this book is the need to interrogate the way in which racism and class have coloured every aspect of our current educational enterprise and have affected the way in which adults approach belonging.

This book is focused on the context and the practice of creating schools as places of belonging. But it does not talk down to those who read this book. Instead, it assumes that if they have taken up the challenge to create schools in which every child feels that they belong, they will see their own experience in many of the vignettes, and they will be called to teach and lead with a compassionate focus on what can be done to live out the principles through daily reflective practice.

About the author

Kathryn Riley lives in Greenwich in South London, close to the River Thames, a river which brought many people to Britain's shores. Born in Manchester, she traces her family roots to the Irish and Jewish diasporas who were forced to leave their homes by the reality or threats of famines, persecution or displacement from the land. Kathryn has benefited from Manchester's aspirations for its young people. Today she is an international scholar whose work bridges policy and practice.

Kathryn began her work in education as a volunteer teacher in Eritrea, later teaching in inner-city schools, before holding political office as an elected member of the Inner London Education Authority (ILEA) and becoming a local authority chief officer. Her international work included two years with the World Bank, heading its Effective Schools and Teachers Group. She has carried out reviews for the World Bank, the OECD and UNICEF on teacher quality, teacher education and accreditation, educational reform and school leadership, partnering with many countries and colleagues in research, policy and development work. The only continent she has yet to work in is Antarctica!

First appointed as a professor in 1993, Kathryn is Professor of Urban Education at UCL Institute of Education, where she has introduced a highly regarded master's degree programme, Leading in Diverse Cultures and Communities. Her past PhD and EdD students now occupy leading positions in education and social policy in many parts of the world.

Kathryn is interested in how to involve staff, young people and their families in school change. Her pioneering approaches to research include training young people to be researchers, and her current focus is on how to create the conditions for school belonging. Through her recent work, she has identified the ways in which new forms of compassionate leadership can help harness the creativity and energy of young people, staff and school communities. She has published widely and has also produced a series of videos on place and belonging,

With DancePoet TioMolina, Kathryn co-founded The Art of Possibilities, which brings together the best of the worlds of education, culture and art to make schools places of welcome and belonging. She is profoundly optimistic about what can be achieved.

Acknowledgements

I have learned much about the importance of place and belonging through the unfailing generosity of spirit and energy of the many friends, colleagues, researchers, students and young people I have met along the way.

Let me begin with a warm appreciation to all the children and young people I have met along the way. I will always hold in my heart the wonderful young people from St Anthony's primary school who referred to me as the 'belonging lady', and who, through their video on 'belonging', taught me about the rich legacy children can leave behind when they move on to another phase of their education. Most of the schools, teachers and children referred to in the book have been anonymised. However, the children from St Anthony's are there for you to 'meet' on video: see www.theartofpossibilities.org.uk.

Grateful thanks and appreciation to colleagues associated with the UCL Institute of Education, firstly, my recent research co-researchers, Dr Tracey Allen, Dr Max Coates, Dr Sergio Galdames and Dr Manuela Mendoza. Their ideas have influenced this book. Over the years I have also enjoyed the encouragement and support of Kristyna Campbell, Rhoda Furniss, Professor Toby Greany, Professor Qing Gu, Dr Rupert Higham, Sol Perez Martinez, Dr Dina Mehmedbegovic, Bilan Yusuf and Professor Louise Stoll. Many thanks to Pat Gordon-Smith, Commissioning Editor, UCL Press for her clear stewardship of this book and the wonderful skill she has of pushing you to go even further! I will always appreciate the encouragement of the late Professor Geoff Whitty to come and find a home at the Institute of Education.

I owe much to the schools I have worked with, and to the openness and collaboration of inspiring leaders, including Professor Anita Berlin, Jo Dibb, Claudet Hedman, Heather Loveridge, Dame Mary Marsh, Dr Vanessa Ogden and Lorna White. The circle of friends and colleagues I have worked with has widened through the 3P Network of the International Congress for School Effectiveness and Improvement and includes Anton Florek, Professor Karen Seashore Louis, Boudewijn Van Velzen and Dr Sara Tomiti. Their ideas and energy spur me on. Karen has been a constant source of inspiration for many years, and I offer my sincere thanks to her for her rich and insightful foreword to this book. Anton has become just the chum you need to push your thinking forward.

I have also been privileged to work in close partnership with a number of organisations which are a force for good in terms of equity, belonging and inclusivity. These include the Deptford Challenge Trust (through our project 'Deptford a World of Possibilities'); the National Education Union (particular thanks to Judy Ellerby and Dr Ros McNeil); the Staff College; and many diocesan groups and local authorities, most recently Telford and Wrekin Council, Hackney Council and Islington Council. Particular thanks to the headteachers from these three authorities.

The many partnerships and collaborations I have been involved in across the world have also contributed to the ideas in this book. I would particularly like to thank Dr Kelly-Ann Allen and Professor Kipling D. Williams for their contributions to this book and their insightful perspectives. Kipling is the Distinguished Professor of Psychological Sciences at Purdue University and has been a leading figure in developing understanding about what it means to be ostracised. Kelly-Ann is Senior Lecturer and Educational and Developmental Psychologist, Monash University, Australia. Her particular contribution to the field has been to add to our understanding of the ways in which classroom practices can help create a sense of belonging.

I would also like to express my appreciation to Dr Susanne Sahlin (Sweden), Daniela Figueroa Moya and Dr Carmen Montecinos (Chile), and colleagues from the Departament d'Educació Catalonia. Special thanks to my good friends and colleagues in Morocco, most notably the indefatigable Dr Mohammed Elmeski, Dr Elarbi Imad (Moroccan Center for Civic Education), Abdellah Yousfi, Meriem Benoualiallah and her inspiring school students (Moroccan Association of Teachers of English).

My ideas have also been influenced by a range of writers, thinkers, practitioners and friends, including Dr Tanya Arroba, Michele Costa Lukis, Sean Coughlan, Cindy Dron, John O'Donoghue, Amelia Gentleman, Bob Hope and Richard Rohr. The practical aspects of my work have been supported by Lisa Jo Robinson (with her fresh and original approach to design work) and Kudsi Tuluoglu, who has always provided sterling support for computing and IT.

My family has always been a source of support and inspiration, particularly my parents Agnes and Bernard Riley, and over recent years my daughter Jo Tilley-Riley and my cousin Jane-Anne Riley.

Finally, I would like to acknowledge the significance of Roberto Molina Rivero (DancePoet TioMolina) in shaping my thinking over the last decade. Roberto was my creative partner in 'The Art of Possibilities', and my husband. He challenged and encouraged me in equal measure and taught me to recognise that creating schools which are places of belonging is about connecting the emotions, the intellect and the creative imagination. The invigorating process of drawing out the talents and skills of our young people, and the staff who work with them, is the art of possibilities.

Introduction

The impetus for the book

Belonging is that sense of being somewhere you can be confident that you will fit in, a feeling of being safe in your identity and at home in a place. The 'place' at the heart of this book is school: one of the few shared social institutions that can create a sense of safety and belonging for young people or a sense of exclusion. Yet across many countries and contexts, young people's sense of belonging in school is declining.

This book began life as a critique of the spectacular ways a number of young people had been let down. This was manifested in:

- A lack of recognition of the impact of student exclusion and a sense of not belonging in school on young people, their families and society;
- An over-reliance on a narrow range of performance measures to calibrate education systems;
- The failure of policymakers to act on the evidence about the benefits to young people of school belonging (Riley 2019a).

The book covers the two sides of the 'belonging' story. The first is the dispiriting one which is reflected in the unacceptable state of affairs which characterise many school systems: rising levels of unhappiness; growing rates of exclusion from school; ongoing increases in mental health and wellbeing issues for many young people. The other side of the story is a profoundly optimistic one and is based on compelling evidence about the strong relationship between young people's sense of belonging in school and their happiness, confidence and academic performance. As the book evolved, and the weight of this evidence grew, so did my optimism.

Optimism is a powerful tool for change. In *The Upswing* Robert Putnam (2020) examined social, political and historical lessons from nineteenth-century America: the shift from an 'I' individualistic society, to a communitarian 'we' society, and back again to the 'me' agenda.

Arriving at his optimistic assessment about the future, he concluded that the disarray and polarisation which had come to characterise American society could turn into an 'upswing': a society less based on self-interest and more grounded on generosity.

Putnam completed *The Upswing* before the Covid-19 pandemic emerged and sent a shockwave around the globe. Yet the pandemic also holds within it the seeds of new possibilities. Many certainties have gone, and the evidence presented in the book suggests that new thinking is emerging about how to lead schools and build connections with communities in ways that will encourage young people to feel safe in their own skin and comfortable in their identity: to feel that they belong.

Writing about the Covid-19 pandemic, Yuval Harari reminds us that 'the storm will pass' and 'humankind . . . survive . . . [yet] we will inhabit a different world' (Harari 2020: 1). The question is: what will that world be like? The decisions governments make during a crisis will shape the world to come. The choices we make as educators will influence the lives of future generations.

How we think and how we talk changes what we see as being possible. This book's narrative is about possibilities: schools as places of connectiveness, belonging and agency. *Compassionate Leadership for School Belonging* offers evidence-based ideas, applicable to many countries and contexts, about the *why*, *how* and *what* of school belonging. Today's narrative – and today's questions – will shape tomorrow's realities.

In a global climate of volatility, made even more uncertain by the Covid-19 pandemic: why do schools need to be places of belonging? How can we make them great places to be where children and young people can feel at home in their own skin? And what needs to change for this to happen?

Asking the questions that matter: beginning with 'why'?

The book's jumping off point is the 'why': *why* schools need to be places of belonging. Simon Sinek (2009) argues that while many organisations can tell you 'what' they do, it is the best organisations and leaders who start with 'why' they are doing what they are doing. He offers compelling examples of how much more can be achieved if we remind ourselves to start everything by asking 'why'.

Asking the 'why' question about school belonging forces us to acknowledge the scale of the contemporary problems with exclusion and a sense of not belonging. It leads us to recognise that schools are one of the few points of continuity and stability in the lives of the growing number of young people for whom home and community are not fixed.

Ultimately, asking the 'why' question takes us to what matters – the intentions, dreams and aspirations which will bring others on board. It is not logic in any organisation that inspires loyalty or builds trust, Sinek argues, but hopes and beliefs.

If schools were places of belonging, more young people would experience a sense of school connectedness, have friends and opportunities, perform better academically and come to believe that their teachers care about them, their learning and their future. They would find themselves in a space where they could develop their sense of self, identity and agency. Their teachers would feel more professionally fulfilled, and their families accepted. Asking the 'why' question about school belonging paves the way for a journey inspired by shared beliefs and a sense of possibilities.

The 'how' and 'what' questions follow on from the 'why'. How can we change the attitudes and expectations which are holding young people back? What support do policymakers, school leaders and classroom leaders who develop policies and practices need in order to create the conditions for school belonging, at different levels of the school system?

In searching for answers to these questions, I have drawn on key conceptual issues – such as agency and social capital – to explain connections. I have also homed in on three significant concepts which best describe the policy and practice ingredients needed to make significant and positive changes. These are:

- *Intentionality*: Taking purposeful actions in response to contemporary challenges about belonging and exclusion.
- *Connectivity*: Developing collaborations with families, communities and other schools to build connections and change existing patterns of behaviour and relationships.
- *Communication*: Taking steps to include many different voices and listening to and engaging them with compassion.

The scope of the book

Compassionate Leadership for School Belonging offers a contemporary narrative about leadership as a compassionate activity aimed at creating the conditions for school belonging. The compassionate leaders who can make a difference are found in classrooms and in formal leadership positions in schools, as well as in a range of policymaking roles.

The book's evidence-based arguments are presented in many forms. Qualitative evidence is woven into the text, offering insights into complex issues around school belonging: what it feels like to be excluded, ostracised, to not belong – and what it feels like to belong. This is supported by the power of analytical data which is presented in many forms, including the OECD's analysis of patterns of student alienation across countries, and findings from a range of quantitative research studies. The first broad conclusion from the evidence reported in the book is that a sense of school connectedness and belonging has positive health and education benefits (social, emotional and academic), and the second is that the conditions for school belonging are created through purposeful, connected and compassionate approaches.

In reporting on my own research on place and belonging, I have drawn on 10 studies carried out between 2001 and 2021. You will find a synthesis of these in Appendix 1 alongside descriptions of the collaborative and qualitative research methods and tools used. These methodologies include training young people and newly qualified teachers to become co-researchers, in the three-year study 'School: A Place Where I Belong?' (Study 3, Appendix 1; Riley 2017).

A range of tools have been used in these studies, including drawing exercises with young people (designed to provide deeper understanding about their life in school and in the community), and card-sort exercises (derived from the literature in the field about belonging), which have been used with teachers to help understand what belonging means to them, personally and professionally. Of the 10 studies listed in Appendix 1, headteachers, principals and senior school leaders were involved in eight; children and young people in six; agencies working in education, health and social policy in four; teachers and support staff in three; families and communities also in three; and local system leaders in two.

The book also includes insightful research summaries from two leading academics, Dr Kelly-Ann Allen and Professor Kipling D. Williams, as well as vignettes which illustrate significant issues from different vantage points and perspectives. Some of these vignettes are my own stories. Stories reveal what is often hidden: the impact of an event on an individual, on their families and on their communities. Stories are data of a different kind. They touch us and reach us in ways that can help us understand what it means to belong, or to feel excluded. It is often the story, the person behind the data, which inspires the change and makes the difference.

The organisation of the book

The book is divided into three parts, each subdivided into three chapters. It begins with this overview and ends with a final reflection. Further details about the research covered in the book and illustrations of research activities are included in the appendices. The structure is as follows.

Part 1 introduces the global and contextual factors which make school belonging such a critical issue in today's uncertain world. In Chapter 1, the discussion about the importance of schools as places of belonging is located in the context of the Covid-19 pandemic and a world in which the displacement of people and communities has become a daily occurrence. The walls between school and communities are porous and the chapter highlights some of the challenges facing young people today, as well as the interplay between the world on the streets and the world in the classroom. Past events (the 1981 Brixton Riot) and contemporary realities (the Windrush scandal which erupted in 2018) are used to illustrate the significance of these connections and the implications for school belonging. Belonging is a complex experience and emotion, triggered by a range of factors, and can shift rapidly into 'not belonging', with damaging consequences for individuals and society.

Chapter 2 draws on both quantitative and qualitative data to examine the many ways in which young people can become ostracised or excluded. Three themes are explored: (i) the broad trends, including the rise in young people's sense of not belonging in school; (ii) what it means to be on the outside looking in and at the receiving end of such negative experiences as bullying, racism, sexism or homophobic attitudes; and (iii) the scale and impact of exclusion and its disproportionate impact on particular groups of young people, including black boys and young people living in poorer communities.

Chapter 3 offers a research overview of key evidence about school belonging and summarises the broad weight of data which shows a strong relationship between young people's sense of belonging in school and their happiness, confidence, academic performance and sense of personal agency. The chapter illustrates how engaging teachers and young people as researchers in collaborative forms of inquiry can help build school belonging (Riley 2017). Asking the question 'Is our school a place where everyone feels they belong?' encourages both teachers and young people to recognise and enact their agency.

Part 2 explores how trust between school and communities can help grow school belonging; illustrates what school belonging looks like; and offers tools which can be used to help build school belonging. Schools which are successful in creating a sense of school belonging are closely attuned to their communities and neighbourhoods. Chapter 4 illustrates what this means in practice, and ways in which sharing knowledge and understanding between schools and communities helps build trust. When schools recognise the importance of local communities and take steps to build on the strengths of those communities, roots and connections are built. Mutual understanding enables schools to provide the physical and emotional spaces and opportunities within school that can engage young people in a process of building belonging and community.

Drawing on findings from research commissioned by the National Education Union (NEU) on the links between a sense of belonging, behaviour and learning outcomes, Chapter 5 identifies the characteristics of schools where 'belonging' works. These features include supportive behaviour polices; strong and positive teacher–student relationships; and shared aspirations. In schools where belonging 'works', young people feel visible, valued and do well. Teachers know they can make a difference and parents experience a sense of welcome. School leaders set a climate of possibilities through their compassionate focus on people.

The practice-oriented Chapter 6 offers a range of conceptual tools, lenses and key concepts, to help deepen understanding about how school belonging is conceptualised, experienced and enacted. These perspectives can also be used to identify potential trigger points such as the changes in day-to-day practices or the leadership actions which can make a difference, or the policy shifts needed to create a positive climate. The chapter is framed around the notions of ways of thinking, ways of understanding and ways of locating. For each of these three elements, sense-making tools or linked concepts are introduced to illustrate the theme.

Part 3 reflects on the complex challenges facing school leaders and introduces the 'Three Cs Framework' of compassion, connectivity and communication as a way of thinking about how to bring together the leadership, policy and practice dynamics needed to recast 'what is' into 'what can be'.

How school leaders think, decide and respond to challenging events, and the degree to which they draw on their personal and professional knowledge to create a roadmap of possibilities, is critical to the wellbeing of children and adults, and their sense of belonging and agency. Chapter 7 illustrates the ways in which the pressures associated with leading schools in demanding socio-economic contexts, and at times of unexpected and extreme trauma, can put leaders' values, beliefs and practices to the test. The 'Three Cs Framework' (a highly relational and compassionate and place-based form of leadership, driven by deep wells of compassion) is introduced, as a way of mapping the elements of leadership required to create the conditions for school belonging.

Chapter 8 continues the exploration of leadership by reporting on findings from a collaborative research inquiry, 'Leading in a New Era', which was undertaken during the Covid-19 pandemic, between April 2020 and January 2021. The study brought together 16 headteachers in three localities in the UK at a time of huge challenges which generated significant pressures for them as school leaders. The chapter explores their responses to these challenges and revisits the 'Three Cs Framework', going deeper into what it means to be a compassionate leader, and exploring whether the framework's core elements offer a viable approach to leadership which can help put schools on a pathway to belonging.

In reframing 'what is' and recasting this into 'what can be', the final chapter steps away from the immediacy of the data to look at the wider landscape and reflect on the conditions needed to create school belonging. This ambitious approach is based on a 'mindset of possibilities' and represents a move away from the *transactional* (here are the results we need to get) to the *aspirational* (here is what we can do to enable young people to fulfil themselves and contribute to society). Points of intervention and action in policy and practice are identified across the education system which can make a significant difference, in an approach characterised by intentionality, consistency and connectivity.

The final reflection brings together some key elements of the belonging story which have unfolded in this book, reinforcing the message that wisdom and compassion can help build connections and communities, and create the conditions for school belonging.

Part 1
Why school belonging matters

1
Searching for a place

> To be rooted is perhaps the most important and least recognised need of the human soul . . . uprootedness is by far the most dangerous malady to which human societies are exposed. (Weil 2002 [1952]: 54)

This chapter is painted on a wide canvas which touches on the uprootedness and uncertainty that characterise the lives of so many young people today. The spotlight is on the world beyond the classroom, the uncertainty which characterises the lives of many young people, and how events which take place outside school seep through into the classroom. The desperate search of families for a place to belong can be found in many countries and contexts and the chapter begins with a story (Vignette 1) about a boy called Abdi about his search for a place to belong.

Vignette 1: Abdi – the boy from Burundi who found his place of belonging in a school in Sweden

It is the autumn of 2019. Cuban DancePoet TioMolina and I have been invited to work with two primary schools. Their names are Breckon Hill Primary in Middlesbrough (a post-industrial town in North Yorkshire) and Hellbergsskolan in Sundsvall, a comfortable farming town and seaport in northern Sweden: two towns which on the face of it have little in common.

However, the similarities between the histories of the children in the classrooms of these two schools are striking. Children from Syria, Iraq, Eastern Europe; children from areas of conflict in Africa (Ethiopia, Burundi, Somalia); children from communities on the move, such as Czech Roma. Young people with similar stories to tell can be found in classrooms in many parts of the world: London,

Minneapolis, Sydney. Happenstance, movements of population, the responses of governments to the plight of refugees can change classrooms in the blink of an eye.

We begin by running workshops for the children about place, belonging and identity. TioMolina uses spoken word, poetry with music and dance, to perform *Yo Soy el Punto Cubano* ('I am the essence of Cuba'), a song written by Cuban singer-songwriter Celina González, a Grammy Award winner, and later recorded by Celia Cruz. The music is of the Cuban countryside and evokes a sense of love and nostalgia for home. We use this to lead into a discussion with the children about home, and what it feels like to belong in their school. They talk about feeling safe, being themselves, having fun and trying out new things.

I ask the children: 'What does TioMolina feel about Cuba?' In Breckon Hill Primary, Mariama from Syria tells us, 'He feels he belongs there. It's a good feeling.' In Hellbergsskolan, Abdi from Burundi responds to the same question and replies, 'He can be himself.' Over a pleasant lunch at Hellbergsskolan, with staff and pupils sitting and chatting amiably together in typical Swedish school style, I ask Abdi, 'What do you like about Sweden?' His response is simple and immediate: *No one is fighting here. When I leave my house, no one is trying to kill me.*

And there in the starkest of terms is the reality of his life and why schools need to be places of belonging, as Hellbergsskolan is for Abdi.

In our world on the move, wealth and status are no protection against becoming a refugee, against the loss of home at the hand of the despot. As Benjamin Zephaniah declaims in 'We refugees', a poem which TioMolina also performs at the two schools with the help of the children, 'We can all be refugees . . . / We can be hated by someone / For being someone' (Zephaniah 2016: 33).

Breckon Hill Primary and Hellbergsskolan are united by the impact of global events, and by the ways in which they have responded with open hearts to children who have experienced events many of us can scarcely comprehend. For these children and their families, their schools have become their places of belonging in a troubled world.

Place and placeness

French philosopher Simone Weil captured the ache of not belonging created by a lack of roots and connections. She came to conclude that the antidote to 'uprootedness' and 'placelessness', that loss of identity and cultural security experienced by vulnerable urban dwellers (Eade 2000; Hague and Jenkins 2005), was a sense of place and belonging.

Schools are communities, 'political entities' in which young people learn how to become part of society (Alexander 2013). Whether young people feel they belong in school influences how they think about themselves today, and how they see their future on our planet as global citizens. Abdi's story reminds us why place and belonging matter, and why schools need to be places of belonging.

Young people's sense of belonging in school is shaped by what they bring to it – their histories, their day-to-day lived realities – as well as schools' practices and expectations. A 10-year-old student-researcher who was part of a team involved in researching school belonging (described more fully in Chapter 4) told me, 'If children don't belong in schools, they don't belong anywhere' (Riley 2017: 90). While schools' policies, practices and expectations enable or constrain young people, the focus of this chapter is on the interplay between the world on the streets and the world in the classroom, in creating a sense of school belonging, or exclusion.

Our world is full of boundless promise and possibilities. Yet it is also a world in which more people are on the move – dislodged, dislocated, placeless – than at any other time since the end of the Second World War. Half of them are children (UNHCR 2015). Abdi's story signposts the realities behind those figures: the ways in which global factors loom large and emergencies can transcend borders, touching the everyday fabric of school life.

We live in a globalised world which has witnessed what Zygmunt Bauman has described as a shift from *solid* times (when people knew their place, good and bad) to *liquid* times which are fluid and unbounded (Bauman 2006). Uncertainty characterises the lives of many children and young people, and the growing sense of social isolation which emerged during the Covid-19 pandemic, coupled with the fears of many young people about what is 'going down' on the street, all serve to reinforce the importance of place and belonging.

Searching for a place

The notion of place is a powerful one: the place where we are from, the place where we live, the place we would like to be. It signifies issues about identity and belonging (or the lack of it), and about roots and connections (or the lack of them) and about being the insider or the outsider. Place is both a physical reality and an emotional response to the world around us, and the power of place and belonging resonates in many ways. Animals mark their terrain. Gangs assert their territory. Place takes on a particular meaning for those who have become unwilling exiles, members of the world's many diasporas – forced by economic, political or social factors beyond their control to leave their homes.

The search for belonging is a strong human emotion which drives many of our actions. In the 1940s, American psychologist Abraham Maslow argued that all humans have a set of primal human needs, including for love and belonging (Maslow 1943). More recently, Ivan Tyrell and Joe Griffin (2013) have expanded Maslow's list of five basic human needs to nine. Their list includes having fun and feeling that life is enjoyable; feeling safe and secure from day to day; and having a sense of some control and influence over life's events. This is more of a 'cocktail' of essential requirements than a hierarchy, as Maslow had suggested (Coates 2018), but their analysis reinforces the importance of belonging and feeling part of a place, part of a community.

The search for place is expressed in the yearning of the diasporas for home: a feeling captured so vividly in the work of Irish playwright Brian Friel. Michael, the central character in Friel's play *Dancing at Lughnasa*, looks back to the summer of his youth, remembering how his mother and her sisters had step-danced with abandonment and joy, like the excited schoolgirls of their youth (Friel 1990). By the end of the play, the family has become divided and two of the sisters have departed for London, never to be seen again.

So many of our own family stories are about place and belonging. They remind us of who we are, the places which are important to us or our families, our own feelings about belonging. The question 'where are you from?' can be a positive and inclusive invitation, a way of eliciting something about a person's sense of identity and making a connection. It can also be a test: a way of separating people and pinpointing the insiders and the outsiders.

The 'belonging' stories for my family – drawn from the Irish and Jewish diasporas – were about finding a place for themselves in Manchester: a city which offered a damp but grudging welcome, and the chance of work in the cotton mills of yesteryear. My answer to the question 'where are you from?' is usually along the following lines: 'I'm from Manchester but I live in London.' If the conversation 'grows up', I might talk about my tribe (Lancashire Irish), or even describe some of the behavioural characteristic of that tribe as I was growing up: Labour voting, Manchester United supporting, Catholic by birth. Prompted further, I may add that I was born in Wythenshawe, then a predominantly white working-class estate and one of the largest social housing developments in the UK, which sprung up as part of the regeneration following the Second World War.

In the aftermath of that war, my family moved to Wythenshawe for a fresh start. They exchanged bomb sites and life in an impoverished city centre for a semi-rural idyll: new houses and the novelty of indoor toilets ('loos', as we called them). There were open spaces. The schools had large playing fields. As a family we had no heirlooms to store, or capacious garrets in our country estates to deposit them in. However, we did have the security of knowing something about the traditions and roots of our ancestors, as well as the tough challenges they had faced. The stories we stored in our memories – as our parents, cousins, aunties and uncles got together over many a celebration – became the roots and branches of our identity. Over the years, those stories have helped me find my place in the world, to locate myself in my adopted city of London, and maintain my Mancunian identity and my own sense of belonging. Not everyone is so lucky today.

In today's world, those with the greatest needs struggle to find a sense of place and belonging. Failing to find it in one place, many search further afield. In a book evocatively entitled *A Bed Called Home*, Mamphela Ramphele (1993) captured the struggle for home, place and belonging for South Africa's migrant workers. As hostel dwellers in spartan and overcrowded buildings in Cape Town, their only personal space was their bed. As they struggled to keep a tenuous hold on this one physical space, their sense of self, identity and belonging slowly diminished.

Tim Creswell investigated the development of New York's Lower East Side, exploring how the area came to be home to a succession of immigrant communities: Irish, Jewish, Italian, Eastern European, Haitian, German and Puerto Rican (Creswell 2004). He recorded their political struggles, as well as the ways in which the different communities had used the spaces in the Lower East Side to link to their homelands: painting tenement walls in the rich Caribbean colours of coral, turquoise and yellow to evoke memories of home, or creating a Puerto Rican community centre in the style of a 'casita', a small single-storey

Latin American house which they decorated with the national flag. He concluded that a sense of place and belonging was a central element of the human psyche, a 'bedrock of human meaning and social relations' (Creswell 2004: 32).

In a global context in which social and economic divisions are widening (Putnam 2015), and humanitarian disasters 'threaten' the lives and futures of many (UNICEF 2017), young people's hold on their sense of place today can be as fragile as for those new arrivals to New York. That fragility is evident in the lives of the 150 million young people in the Global South who have experienced conflicts and displacement crises, or the devastation of seasonal storms (UNICEF 2017). In the Global North, young homeless people have found themselves caught up in the growing problem of labour and sex trafficking across North America. Based on interviews with more than 600 homeless young people, across 10 cities in the US and Canada, researchers from Loyola University found that one in five had been subject to some form of human trafficking (Murphy 2017). North and South meet when young people from Vietnam find themselves trafficked to the UK to service cannabis farms (Gentleman 2017).

On the streets and inside the classrooms

The walls that divide schools from the realities of life in the surrounding communities are porous. My own experience of living and teaching in South London in the late 1970s and early 1980s opened my eyes to the significance of the relationship between the school and the local community. My first teaching job in the UK was at Peckham Girls' School, a large comprehensive school of some 1,500 students in South London, housed in a sprawling glass edifice which turned into a hothouse during the summer months. Later I moved to Lavender Hill School Battersea, not far from Brixton. The neighbourhood around Peckham Girls' was a fluid and relatively impoverished area in which families faced many social and economic challenges. Today, while it remains a highly diverse neighbourhood, it is also a place on the move, with its own locally brewed 'Little Bird Gin'.

In January 1981, a fire occurred at a house party in nearby New Cross, taking the lives of 13 young black people. Pupils from the school I was working in had friends, cousins and neighbours who had attended the party. Emotions were high and in the weeks that followed, there were protests about police brutality and the lack of progress in establishing who had started the fire. Investigators were later to conclude that the fire had been started deliberately. No charges have ever been made in relation to the fire.

The instruction to staff from the school's senior management was that teachers were not to discuss the fire, an instruction reiterated when the Brixton Riot erupted later in the year. These events were viewed as being beyond the school's jurisdiction and too difficult and complex to engage with. The boundaries dividing the school from local communities were impenetrable – and not to be crossed.

The Brixton Riot unfolded over a three-day period and was an eruption of anger about the racism which had been bubbling beneath the surface for many years (Riley 1982). At the time, I was carrying out research for my PhD on race and gender issues and my late husband, John Tilley, was the MP for Brixton. During the riot, his time was taken up with fielding phone calls from the worried parents of young black people who had been scooped up off the street to be held in police custody and trying to talk to police command and local community leaders about a possible way through the impasse.

The riot had begun with increasingly intense stand-offs between police and local people about heavy police methods. Rumours were rife. Anxiety was in the air and as light faded, the stand-offs turned into confrontation. By nightfall, the sky was illuminated by flames and the air polluted by the smell of the acrid fumes from burning vehicles. Such images filled TV screens for some weeks, as politicians and pundits sought to lay blame, or make sense of what had happened.

In response to the riots, the prime minister of the day, Margaret Thatcher, roundly dismissed the idea that unemployment and racism had been contributory factors ('No, I don't somehow think that is the primary cause. After all, we had much higher unemployment in the 1930s, but we didn't get this behaviour in any way') or that the local population had lost their trust in a police force which had behaved 'like an army of occupation': 'What absolute nonsense and what an appalling remark and I condemn the person who made it . . . [The police protected] the citizens in Lambeth to the very best of their ability' (ITN 1981).

She went on to appoint Lord Scarman, a senior judge, to lead the inquiry into the causes of the riot. His excoriating report proved to be a significant challenge to the establishment of the day, unearthing as it did the impact of years of limited employment opportunities, including the disproportionate and indiscriminate use of 'stop and search' powers by the police against black people (Scarman 1981). This was the first time that a government report had spoken of institutional racism. Files released some 25 years later included a handwritten note by Mrs

Thatcher: 'I'm afraid the (Scarman) Report seems highly critical of the police' (BBC News 2014).

The 1981 Scarman Inquiry and the Rampton Report (1981) of the same year (which looked at the educational experiences of West Indian children) both drew attention to the impact of racism in schools. Two incidents described in those reports remain with me and are summarised here.

The first incident, adapted from Scarman, took place in February 1981. The setting is a large multiracial school in Brixton.

> *M. is black and a former pupil. He revisits the school to keep an appointment with a member of staff. A senior teacher who is new to the school, and therefore unaware that he is talking to a former pupil, calls the police because, as he put it later, the boy did not show 'due deference'. When the police arrive, M. is in the tuck shop in the company of the member of staff with whom he had an appointment. He is pulled out of the shop and pinned to the ground by several policemen. At one point there are 13 policemen in the school playground. This all takes place in front of young, impressionable pupils, waiting to buy goods from the tuck shop.*

The second incident is from the Rampton Inquiry. The date is November 1981 and the setting is a teacher training institute in the Home Counties.

> *A fourth-year BEd student stops her sociology lecturer to speak to her. 'I very much enjoyed the book you lent me on black women in Britain. There is one thing I am worried about: are Asian women the ones with straight hair or crinkly hair?'*

The issue was not about *whether* racism existed in schools but about *who* brought it through the school gates.

I carried out the fieldwork for my PhD research in the late 1970s and early 1980s, which gave me the opportunity to look into the playgrounds and classrooms of three London schools: two single-sex girls' schools and one coeducational school, all serving relatively disadvantaged communities. In the coeducational school, the girls were marginalised by the school's day-to-day practices and assumptions. At any recreational period, these young women were hidden in the cloakrooms, or could be found sitting in groups in the corners of the hall, or the dining room, or perched at the periphery of the playground areas, particularly on sunny days when the deep shadows gave the boys the opportunity to play a favourite game, 'shadow wanking' (Riley 1985a, 1985b, 1994).

In one of the single-sex schools, the young women of African-Caribbean origin were in a small minority. They typically described themselves as being invisible in the school and marginalised by their encounters with their white peers, and found themselves on the outside looking into a school in which they had little sense of belonging, as the following example illustrates.

> Sometimes they (white girls) ask some silly questions. Because we're black we're different . . . I know we're different . . . We have to put grease on our hair, and they think that's silly. This girl asked me 'how do you curl your hair' and I said 'curlers, what do you think?' I think she thought we used bones or something. (Riley 1994: 66)

Evidence about the degree to which black children have been let down by the British school system began to unfold in the 1970s. In 1971, Bernard Coard published a scathing critique of the British education system, detailing the experiences of children of West Indian origin throughout the 1960s and 1970s (Coard 1971). Teacher expectations were low, he argued, and many young people felt denigrated. The result was that a disproportionate number of boys of African-Caribbean origin found themselves in special schools and were wrongly labelled as 'educationally subnormal', a term from the 1944 Education Act used to define children thought to have limited intellectual ability – and one unlikely to generate a sense of school connectedness and belonging.

As a teacher, researcher, and in the 1980s an elected member for education in London, I began to see the ways in which racism, sexism and dismissive attitudes can creep into the life of a school, leading young people to feel invisible and on the periphery of a school life in which they have no part to play. In Chapter 3, I take these issues forward, examining contemporary data about school exclusion (and its impact on young black people); evidence of the rise in the number of young people who feel that they do not belong in school; and information about the increase in sexual harassment and abuse in schools and colleges.

Young people's lives

Over the years, I have tried to understand something of young people's lives both inside and outside school. On a typical school visit, I ask the children and young people I meet, 'Do you feel you belong in this school?' If they have experienced a sense of belonging, they reply with alacrity, with such comments as:

I feel safe here.
They know who I am.
I know they like me.
I'm different but I can be me in this school.
Belonging means that you're not just left out and lonely.

Children from an international school in The Hague responded to this 'belonging' question by writing and performing a belonging song, a collective act of belonging. The chorus ran as follows: 'I belong when I float through the air, peaceful and calm, when I belong'.

However, for many young people, particularly those on the margins of society, the world can feel an unsafe place. Encountering social and physical barriers can be a daily occurrence. The Covid-19 pandemic has added to the fragility of the lives of many young people and reminded us of the centrality of schools in their lives, as I had discovered some time earlier through the research project 'Leadership of Place'.

The research focused on young people growing up in impoverished communities in the US, the UK and South Africa (Study 3, Appendix 1; Riley 2013a), and was later extended to Chile (Study 4, Appendix 1; Riley, Montecinos and Ahumada 2016) and Jamaica. The aim was to understand something of the contextual realities of life for children and young people living in impoverished areas, and what it meant to be a school leader in those contexts.

As a prompt for the nearly 200 young people who contributed to that research, I used a drawing tool based on earlier work (Study 1, Appendix 1; Riley and Rustique-Forrester 2002), asking two questions: 'What's it like living round here?' and 'What's it like being in this school?' This exercise proved to be an invaluable instrument for gaining insights into the contrasting realities of everyday life. For the young Londoner who drew Figure 1.1, the many 'good' things in her life included 'free bus passes 4 youths', her school and her 'mates'. However, there were also violent and disturbing aspects in her life, such as gangs and stabbings.

Life on the streets or in the 'barrios' of Chile could be equally tough. Many young people report that they live in daily fear of the drug dealer on their doorstep (Naicker, Chikoko and Mthiyane 2014). The young Chilean student who drew Figure 1.2 lived in a shanty town and told us that when she arrived back home from school, she locked herself in her home to keep herself safe from the drug dealer on the stairwell outside (Study 4, Appendix 1; Riley, Montecinos and Ahumada 2016).

Many of the illustrations from 'Leadership of Place' showed stark and competing realities: areas which were safe and welcoming and

Figure 1.1 My life, good and bad (London, England). Source: author.

Figure 1.2 'I don't like the criminals who threaten me, or the garbage in the streets' (Chile). Source: author.

Figure 1.3 My life inside and outside school (London, England). Source: author.

others which were 'no go'. Figure 1.3, drawn by another young Londoner, is an example of this.

On the right-hand side of the drawing is the neighbourhood: an area characterised by crime, danger, gangs. An open area (the local common) is experienced as a dangerous space, unsafe to walk through, particularly at night. Yet within what is an otherwise bleak external environment, this young woman also relishes the warm embrace of family and culture. In marked contrast to the external realities, school (the left-hand side of the drawing) is a place in which your 'voice' is heard, and you have a chance to be yourself and develop your creativity.

While the research revealed the degree to which school could be a place of possibility, support, friendship and opportunities, travelling to and from your school might be a hazardous experience, as is illustrated in Figure 1.4. In Kingston, Jamaica, you might be 'red-eyed' by someone who was jealous of you ('hey boy, come yah') or you might witness a shooting (the right-hand side of the drawing). In contrast, school could be a place that offered food and provided important opportunities for learning (the left-hand side of the drawing).

In South Africa, the research on leadership of place was carried out in seven schools in Fort Beaufort School District, an impoverished rural area in the heart of the Eastern Cape Province. Drugs and violence

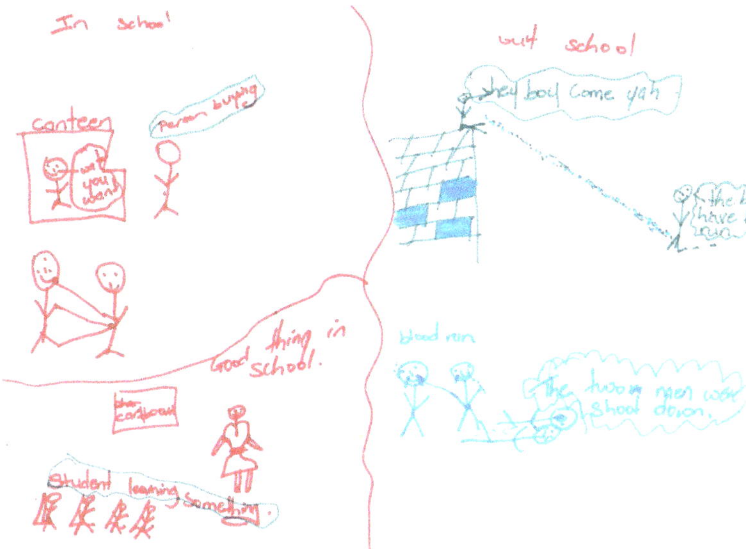

Figure 1.4 On my way to school (Kingston, Jamaica). Source: author.

plagued the neighbourhoods surrounding the schools. Unemployment was high and illness endemic, with up to one in five young people infected with HIV/AIDS. Many children were looked after by their siblings or grandparents while their parents sought employment elsewhere – Port Elizabeth, Johannesburg and Cape Town – perhaps living in the kinds of hostels described by Mamphela Ramphele (1993). I worked with more than 100 young people whose lives were challenging and complex, yet they undertook the drawing exercise with alacrity. They wanted to show me their world.

At Themba High School, a major storm had damaged classroom roofs, wrecking the sewage system. This had deprived the learners of an 'ablution block' and left the school grappling with leaky roofs and broken windows. While some young people expressed concerns about their fellow students ('I don't like . . . the children that don't like school, so there's bad children, like boys who do smoking and do not do homework'), for most, the school was a beacon of opportunity: 'The good thing about my school is . . . You are given an opportunity to express your feelings; you even learn some things you didn't know; if you have a problem you can talk to your teacher about it; teachers are so understanding.'

Crime was a neighbourhood reality – and seemed to pay. Penisi, a Year 10 student from Themba, captured this in his drawing (Figure 1.5)

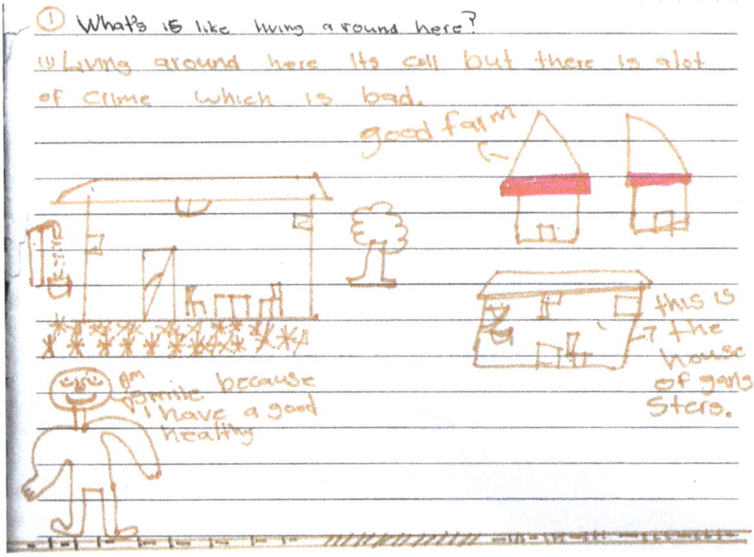

Figure 1.5 The 'smart' house (Eastern Cape, South Africa).
Source: author.

which he explained to me in the following terms: 'That's me, I'm smiling because I have a good health.' In answer to the question about what it was like living around there he wrote, 'Living round here is cool but there is a lot of crime which is bad but there are some good farms.' On the right of the drawing is the 'smart' house. 'This is the house of the gangsters.'

Penisi's description of the 'smart' house took me back to a school I had visited in Belfast as part of earlier research (Study 2, Appendix 1; Riley 2007, 2008). That school also served an impoverished community, this time in a city divided along sectarian lines. As I looked down at the area surrounding the school from the second floor, I was struck by the apparent disparities of poverty and wealth. Many houses were dilapidated, marked out by poverty. Some were freshly painted, the affluence of the owners reflected in the large extensions and expensive cars peeking out of lattice-roofed carports. I asked the school's principal why there was such a difference. The gleaming houses belonged to the local drug dealers, he told me.

Young people know what is 'going down' in their communities and in the neighbourhoods in which they live. They know when uncertainty is in the air. They encode 'social tensions' about global matters, and pick up on 'the stress and anger' of the adults around them about contemporary events (Rethinking Schools 2017: 4). Snippets of news from families and friends combine with the 24-hour buzz of social media to give them a patchwork understanding of the world around them.

The final section of this chapter offers a contemporary example of the ways in which external events can change consciousness about who are the insiders and outsiders in society. The degree to which particular communities are recognised and accepted, and have a sense of belonging, shapes the expectations and beliefs of young people from those communities. They bring these experiences and expectations with them, as they enter the school gate. The story of the Windrush generation which is to follow exemplifies this.

The Windrush generation

The most significant wave of immigrants from the Caribbean to Britain landed in 1948. The first ship to dock was called the *Empire Windrush*, and its passengers, and their families, had been invited to the UK as citizens to help rebuild the nation after the devastation of the Second World War. These new arrivals worked in hospitals, kept transport systems running, enriched the nation's cultural life and battled with overt and incipient racism in a country in which they had a right to live.

However, the place where people think they belong can all too quickly become the place from which they are exiled – by war or political upheaval. This experience of separation, alienation and exile can come not just from the hand of the dictator, and seemingly overnight. Changes in the zeitgeist – the norms that shape the culture of the time – can alter realities. Vignette 2 illustrates this by charting something of the story of the Windrush Generation: a story of belonging and not belonging for Caribbean families and their descendants.

Vignette 2: The *Empire Windrush* and a hot July night

It is a hot July night and the start of the London 2012 Olympic Games. The three-hour extravaganza is watched by more than 1 billion people worldwide. The sassy opening ceremony, designed by filmmaker Danny Boyle, seems to signal a country apparently at ease with itself and its diversity. The queen plays a cameo role, encountering James Bond. The National Health Service is celebrated. Past 'wrongs' are 'righted'. A passenger liner is featured, the *Empire Windrush*, the ship which had brought the first wave of immigrants from the Caribbean to British shores in 1948. Its passengers were invited to help rebuild the nation after the devastation of the Second World War. The children and young people who accompanied their parents on that boat, and other boats and planes, came to be known as the Windrush generation, and to think of themselves as British.

British-Jamaican Doreen Lawrence helps carry the Olympic flag at the ceremony. She arrived in England, aged nine, growing up as one of the 'Windrush generation'. The mother of black British teenager Stephen Lawrence, who was murdered in a racist attack in 1993, she waged a long battle for justice following his death. In 1999 the case she had made was reflected in the findings of the Macpherson Inquiry into Stephen's murder, which concluded that institutional racism in the police force had been a critical factor in failure to convict the white men who had attacked him. Now Baroness Lawrence carried the Olympic flag, and had come to symbolise a new British consciousness about racism.

Fast forward to April 2018, when a scandal of epic proportions erupts, as members of the 'Windrush generation' become unwitting casualties of the UK government's hard-line 'hostile environment policy' towards so-called 'illegal' immigrants. The policy was the invention of then home secretary, and later prime minister, Theresa May, and to raise the profile of the policy, large white vans were sent into areas with diverse populations, bearing posters for all to read: 'Are you in the UK illegally? Go home or face arrest. 100 arrests last weekend in your area' (JCWI 2021).

Undocumented migrants, many of whom were the children of the Windrush generation, found themselves denied the use of health services and the right to work. Reaching retirement age in a country in which they thought they belonged, where they had children and grandchildren, where they had attended schools and colleges, lived and worked and paid their taxes, they have become the outsider, the unwanted – the undocumented migrant, the deportee. Were they no longer British? According to the British government – no.

Many thousands – like HGV driver Rupert Everett, who died aged 74, in 2019, having lived in the UK for over 50 years – were wrongly classified as illegal immigrants. In 2021, the parliamentary ombudsman concluded that the Home Office had made repeated errors, wrongly classifying Rupert as an illegal immigrant, taking away his right to work, and threatening him with arrest and deportation to Jamaica, a country he had last visited at age 19. His daughters have spoken of his distress and sense of isolation. Rupert's death has been linked to the stress he experienced from having been labelled an illegal immigrant (Gentleman 2021). A review of the 'hostile environment policy' concluded that the policy had 'contributed to forcing many people into destitution, has helped to foster racism and discrimination, and has erroneously affected people with the legal right to live and work in the UK' (Qureshi, Morris and Mort 2020: 1).

When the place where our families had been invited to help rebuild a nation becomes a place of rejection – as it did in the UK for many of the the Windrush generation – lives and families are torn apart, dreams disappear. This shattering process touches the lives of others, children, grandchildren, friends, neighbours. If our families don't belong in this country, do we belong in this school?

The Windrush scandal continues to play out, raising profound issues about place and belonging; insiders and outsiders; those who have a 'right' to be here and those who do not (Gentleman 2020). These issues loomed large in the divisive Brexit campaign in the run-up to the national referendum in 2016 about membership of the European Union. The increase in the number of hate crimes reported during that period led one newspaper to ask: 'Is Britain Getting Nastier?' (*Big Issue* 2017).

Whoever they are, or wherever they are, young people are not immune to these external realities, although those living in wealthier circumstances are more likely to be protected from the impact. There are many global events and local circumstances which serve to remind us of the fragility of lives: the impact of the Covid-19 pandemic on children and young people in poverty, or those from refugee or migrant families (Children's Society 2020a); the increase in refugee and migrant deaths in the Mediterranean (UNHCR 2021); the civil war and famine in Ethiopia (Gladstone 2021). If there was ever a time that young people were sheltered from national crisis and global uncertainties, those days have long since gone. And if there was ever a time that a sense of school belonging was more important to young people than it is today, those days are long since lost in the mists of time.

2
On the outside looking in

> I try so hard, but I never get higher results like everybody else. What is wrong with me? (A Year 6 child preparing to take his national assessment tests; Riley 2017: 81)

Belonging is a relational, cultural, geographic and dynamic concept, a complex emotion triggered by a range of factors. Belonging can shift rapidly into 'not belonging', with damaging consequences for individuals and society. This chapter focuses on the negative side of the belonging coin: what it feels to be excluded, ostracised, on the outside looking in. Research tells us that a range of factors contribute to young people feeling that they do not belong in school and to their perceptions about why they are on the outside of school life. The chapter brings these issues together under three themes: (i) the broad trends about a sense of not belonging; (ii) the experience of being on the outside looking in; and (iii) the scale and impact of exclusion.

Young people's experiences of school life can be widely different, even within the same school:

- You can meet your friends *or* you can be bullied.
- The physical environment can be conducive to your learning *or* it can be taxing on you as a learner.
- The ecology of relationships can be healthy and caring *or* it can depress and sap your energy.
- The narrative of everyday school life can contribute to the development of your emotional map *or* it can rattle your self-confidence.

As you scrutinise the data, let me encourage you to return to your own experience of school life, and to think about the children and young people behind the statistics, and ask: *why do most children start school with enthusiasm and curiosity, yet many lose interest along the way, or find themselves dismissed, rejected or excluded? Why aren't policymakers grappling with the question of how to create the conditions for school belonging?*

A sense of 'not' belonging: the broad trends

OECD data on school belonging paints a bleak portrait of rejection. Across the 34 high- and middle-income countries which make up the OECD, one in four children feel that they do not belong in school (OECD 2013). This figure is rising and is now nearer to 1 in 3 (OECD 2017, 2019).

Earlier evidence drawn from the 2003 Programme for International Student Assessment (PISA) – which is the OECD's annual survey for calibrating the reading, mathematics and science performance of 15-year-olds across OECD countries – had indicated that across 42 countries, student disaffection with school ranged from 17 to 40 per cent, on average, with one in four adolescents categorised as having low feelings of belongingness and one in five reporting low levels of academic engagement. This analysis was based on data from 8,354 schools and 224,058 15-year-olds (Willms 2003).

Students' sense of belonging in their school has 'weakened considerably between 2003 and 2015 and waned even further between 2015 and 2018' (OECD 2012, 2019: 51). In the PISA 2015 and 2018 studies, students were asked about their sense of belonging in school. The data indicates that between 2015 and 2018, students' sense of belonging deteriorated. For example, the share of students who agreed or strongly agreed with the positive statements, 'I make friends easily at school' and 'I feel like I belong at school', fell by around two percentage points over that period (OECD 2019).

Researchers and policy analysts have offered a number of reasons to explain this growing sense of not belonging. Some have attributed the decline to the increased importance of national and international league tables and the growing pressures on schools to achieve performance targets. In California, for example, teachers have reported feeling caught between meeting the needs of refugee children – many of whom have had limited access to formal education – and satisfying the stringent policy requirements and expectations of school systems (Drake 2017).

In England, there is evidence that the pressure on schools to achieve high test scores has led to an increase in setting, streaming and other forms of 'ability' grouping, including in reception and nursery classes. Teachers have voiced their concerns about the impact of these practices on children's 'confidence, self-esteem, and aspirations' (Bradbury and Roberts-Holmes 2017: 3). Pressurised examination systems appear to have a particular impact on young people from poorer communities. For example, a review of performance data in English schools – which drew on postcode data to make this comparison – indicates that pupils from disadvantaged backgrounds are almost twice as likely as their more advantaged peers to fail mathematics in the national qualification for 15- and 16-year-olds (the General Certificate of Secondary Education) and are also much less likely to be awarded the top grades (Teach First 2019).

Young people's sense of happiness has also declined. According to the UK's Children's Society, it is now at its lowest ebb since 2010, with almost one in five in the UK having seven or more serious problems in their lives, several of which are school-related (Children's Society 2017). Other indicators of unhappiness include a rise in the number of children self-harming, which health experts have attributed to a range of factors, including low body image, fears of abuse and pressures to succeed in school (Campbell 2016). The Covid-19 pandemic has also contributed to this growing sense of unhappiness, with nearly one in five young people aged 10–17 (over 1 million in total) describing themselves as being unhappy and feeling that their choices in life are gradually being eroded (Children's Society 2020b).

OECD analysis offers an external perspective on the school life of Britain's young people, and their unhappiness. While PISA 2018 reveals some improvement in the academic performance of students in England and Wales (with more mixed results for Scotland and Northern Ireland), these results appear to have been achieved at a significant cost to young people's sense of happiness and belonging, as the data which follows illustrates:

- British 15-year-olds were ranked 69th out of 71 for life satisfaction, with boys being the least satisfied.
- They were ranked 70th out of 71 in their likelihood of supporting the statement 'My life has a clear meaning or purpose'.
- The UK was the only country in Europe to have more than half of the young people reporting that they regularly felt sad.
- More than one in four young reported being bullied 'at least a few times per month' (Coughlan 2019; OECD 2020).

However, high performance scores and happiness do not necessarily go hand in hand. Students in Japan and Korea, who according to the OECD benefit from two of the best disciplinary climates of all PISA-participating countries, were 'some of the most dissatisfied with their lives, at least according to their own reports . . . [and] expressed greater fear of failure and were about twice as likely as students in other OECD countries to report that they always feel scared or sad' (OECD 2020: 51).

Commenting on findings from PISA 2018, leading OECD analyst Andreas Schleicher reflected on the relationship between the features of a school system and young people's sense of happiness, arguing that cooperation with peers and good relations with teachers were strongly associated with higher performance and student wellbeing in every school system participating in PISA. Students were more likely to feel that they belonged in school when their peers were more cooperative. However, individual competition is a key feature of the UK schooling system (Schleicher 2019).

On the outside looking in: let me count the ways

There are many ways that children and young people can come to feel that they do not belong in school. Feeling ostracised or socially excluded is one of these. The ancient Greeks operated the practice of ostracism as a way of banishing people from society. The concept is not typically used in discussions about education, yet it can help capture the ways in which both implicit and explicit school practices and assumptions can serve to banish young people, make them feel invisible, and relegate them to the role of outsider.

In 'What it means to be ostracised' (see below), written specially for this book, distinguished professor of psychology Kipling Williams draws on his experience to explain how the process of being ostracised can play out in school life and what this can mean for a child or young person.

What it means to be ostracised – by Kipling Williams

To be ostracised is to be ignored and excluded. This means not being looked at, listened to or noticed. It means not being invited to group activities, within and outside school time. It means feeling invisible and unheard.

My research has shown that the brain reacts to even brief episodes of ostracism – by strangers! – as it does when the body experiences physical pain. It robs the individual of a feeling of belonging, drives down their self-esteem, threatens their sense of control, and renders their life more meaningless and unacknowledged.

Ostracised individuals might go to great lengths to fit in with others, going along with the crowd, often doing things that are inconsistent with their values and beliefs. They might also become provocative, aggressive and violent, anything to get noticed. They know that externalising their anger will get them some control and acknowledgement, even if by doing so they become more disliked. Some do neither, and seek solitude instead, assuring further ostracism by giving no one a chance to include them.

Being ostracised disrupts their motivation and ability to work on complex problems that would be common for schoolwork. It increases risk-taking, and the intention to take drugs or have unprotected sex. Experiencing ostracism for too long increases clinical levels of alienation, depression, helplessness and worthlessness. Those who have experienced long-term ostracism have reported self-harm, suicidal ideation and attempts, promiscuity and eating disorders. It is important to spot students who are all alone and who aren't acknowledged by the other students. Encourage others to involve them in their activities. Look at them. Listen to them. Reach out and be supportive. Even one supportive person can make a difference.

As Kip Williams concludes, 'even one supportive person can make a difference' to a young person's experience of school life. Yet some young people lack even that. A sense of not feeling welcome, the experience of being ostracised, plays out for many young people in the small everyday experiences of school life. Some end up feeling that 'this school doesn't want me' or are fearful that they are not accepted by others (Williams, Forgas and von Hippel 2005). In the year ending March 2020, one in five children aged 10 to 15 in England and Wales experienced at least one type of online bullying behaviour. One in four believed that their school did not deal well with bullying (ONS 2020). In being denied acceptance in school life through bullying, young people also lose out on the richness of learning opportunities.

Bullying is experienced in many different ways and can be linked to racist, sexist and homophobic attitudes. In 2021, the website Everyone's Invited reported that more than 10,000 postings of sexual harassment and abuse of pupils in schools and other education settings had been made over a matter of days. The majority were from students attending prestigious fee-paying schools which are not subject to the same school inspection regimes as state schools. The uproar generated led to concerns about the emergence of UK schools' 'rape culture' (Turner 2021).

In response to this disclosure and the outcry which followed, the UK's Office for Standards in Education, Children's Services and Skills (Ofsted) undertook a review on peer-on-peer sexual harassment and sexual violence. Based on interviews with 900 children and young people in 32 schools and colleges, the conclusion was that sexual harassment was commonplace. Nearly 9 out of 10 girls, and half of boys, had been sent explicit pictures or videos of things they did not want to see, 'a lot or sometimes' (Ofsted 2021). At one school, the girls told inspectors that they could be contacted by up to 10 or 11 different boys a night asking them for nude or semi-nude images (Sellgren and Wills 2021).

The many reasons why young people come to feel alienated, or that they don't belong, are often hidden or unspoken. Menstruation is one example. Depending on family circumstances, menstruation cycles can lead to young women feeling that 'I do not belong in school when I am having my period' – as Figure 2.1 illustrates. Many absent themselves from school for period-related issues, feeling themselves ostracised. Some may struggle on their own with period poverty in school contexts in which menstruation is not normalised or talked about.

Research by Plan International UK (2017) has concluded that 1 in 10 girls are unable to afford sanitary wear; half miss an entire day of school because of their period; and the majority have made up an excuse to avoid going to school. Over the course of a school year, an estimated 140,000 young women in the UK miss school because of period poverty. Lack of access to period products particularly affects refugee and

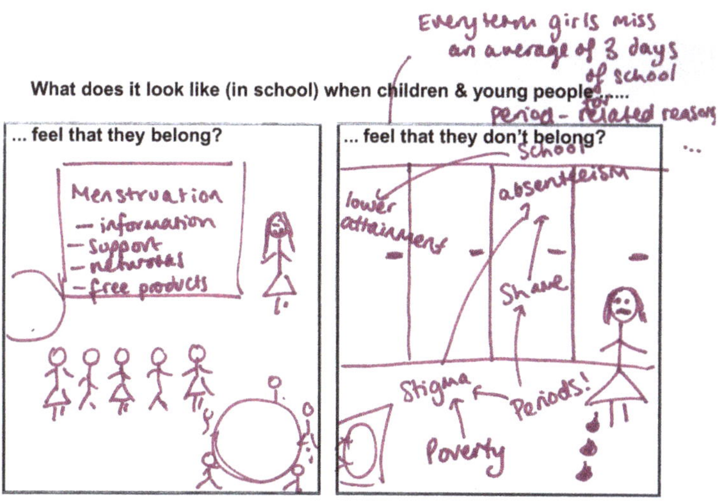

Figure 2.1 There are many ways to be ostracised. Source: author.

asylum-seeking young women (Bloody Good Period and Women for Refugee Women 2019).

A sense of school belonging is linked to acceptance by others. This can be a critical issue for children from refugee families, who may worry about whether others feel that they have a right to be in the country. Yet schools are not always prepared to fully engage with newly arrived communities. In the United States, researchers have argued that too little is known about how young people from refugee families experience schooling (Koyama and Rwehumbiza Bakuza 2017), and that the ways schools engage with their communities can exclude refugee and migrant families, leaving them to find their own spaces to meet and discuss issues outside formal institutions and structures (Das Gupta 2006).

UK organisations have reported that children from refugee families face specific language and cultural barriers which can contribute to a sense of dissonance; difficulties in establishing meaningful personal relationships with other students; and barriers to being understood and respected by their teachers. Young people from refugee families have described their concerns that 'others' do not want them to be in the school and the distress this has caused them (Riley, Mendoza and Gonzales 2020).

The scale and impact of exclusion

Formal exclusion from school is the ultimate red card: the young person is denied membership of the school. School exclusion is both a personal and social issue. Young people from poor communities are twice as likely as their more advantaged peers to feel that they do not belong in school and four times more likely to be excluded (Fair Education Alliance 2017). Researchers have concluded that five times more children are being excluded from school in the UK than official figures indicate, with strong links between school exclusion and social exclusion (Gill, Quilter-Pinner and Swift 2017).

The experience of being excluded from school is a powerful one, as Figure 0.1 demonstrates (see page xiv). This drawing emerged from research on student disaffection conducted some years ago (Study 1, Appendix 1; Riley and Rustique-Forester 2002). The young people involved in the study had all been excluded from school. Their school life had been a fragmented, inconsistent and often lonely experience for them. The bleak image in Figure 0.1 has stayed with me over the years, exemplified in the words 'spoken' by the teachers ('You're stupid', 'You're thick') and the headteacher ('Get out of my school', 'You don't belong here'). The image and the words all convey a deep sense of loss and remind us of the damage that schools can inflict on young people, the magnitude of the problem and the consequences for individuals.

Vignette 3 is about a boy called Kushtrim, who came to England from Albania and found himself excluded from school. It captures the mutual waves of incomprehension that can exist between a young person who has faced tough conditions and the school in which he or she finds themselves. It was told to me by his teacher, Violeta Stabler, a student of mine.

Vignette 3: Kushtrim from Albania, who was excluded from his London school

Kushtrim first came to London as an unaccompanied minor to avoid ethnic conflict at home in Albania. The biggest challenge he faced on his arrival was in adopting more culturally appropriate ways of communicating with people, especially adults in power. In his first year in school, he was quiet and withdrawn and his schoolmates kept their distance. His hardship and suffering were etched on his face.

In Year 11 his English improved and he became loud, outspoken and verbally aggressive. He was popular with students but feared and disliked by teachers. He challenged every school rule, especially those he thought were institutionalising and subjugating him. He wore an Albanian flag and a metal two-headed eagle around his neck and refused to take it off. It was all he had left from his country, the only familiar thing.

By his third year, the choir of the displeased was reaching its crescendo. Nobody noticed that, despite his verbal violence, Kushtrim never laid a finger on anybody. Nobody praised him for mastering English in two years.

The tipping point was when Kushtrim threatened one of the senior staff members. 'If you don't make him leave [school] now, I'll call the police,' the deputy headteacher told his tutor. 'They will pin him down.' The inevitable happened. Kushtrim was excluded from the school, joining the growing ranks of the excluded. Any sense of belonging in the UK was well and truly dissipated.

Over recent years, there have been significant increases in the number of pupils excluded from school. A parallel but equally alienating process to formal exclusions has also taken place in the UK: that of 'offloading' (Hutchinson and Crenna-Jennings 2019). This is a behind-the-scenes practice by which schools pressurise young people unlikely to reach the top grades to leave school. The issue hit the headlines in 2017 when the 'offloading' practices of a seemingly top-performing state school in England (St Olave's Grammar School, Bromley) were exposed (Coughlan 2017; Weale and Fishwick 2017).

The rise in exclusions has been linked to *social stress* (rising child poverty and increases in mental illness); *policy failure* (reduced school funding, a more academic curriculum and a rigorous and highly pressurised accreditation regime); and – in the context of complex and overlapping systems – *systemic dysfunction* (Taylor 2020).

Black students, poor students and those with special educational needs and mental health issues have borne the brunt of exclusions and offloading (Allen, Riley and Coates 2020), and the Timpson Review of school exclusion in England concluded that a disproportionately higher level of temporary and permanent exclusions took place among specific groups of black students (Department for Education 2019). Research also indicates that behaviour management systems which rely on exclusions are more common in schools with higher proportions of black and minority ethnic students and in those located in socio-economically disadvantaged areas (Lacoe 2015): a finding which is a stark reminder of the relationship between exclusion and social inequity.

Kushtrim did not fit into the norms of school life. He had no sense of belonging in the school and was let down by an overstretched and pressurised system. It could have been different. Imagine an alternative scenario.

On Kushtrim's arrival at the school, a training session was conducted with his teachers and information given about the circumstances which had brought him to the UK. Staff came to recognise that linguistic and communicative competence are different. His tutor helped him understand that threatening behaviour would be taken very seriously and said to him, 'Why don't you put your Albanian eagle closer to your heart – under your shirt?' Throughout his time in school, staff kept up regular communication with his guardian and social services and managed to build a trustful relationship with him. The outcome was that Kushtrim took seven GCSEs and went to college to become an electrician. His dream was to drive home to Tirana (adapted from Riley 2103a: 1).

Young people, such as Kushtrim, who are excluded from school are exposed to exploitation; their access to education becomes limited; and they are more likely to be caught up in crime than their peers. Expelled from school, they find themselves at risk of being 'preyed upon' by drug gangs, according to England's chief inspector of schools (Savage 2020).

The disaffected and excluded search for 'belongingness' elsewhere, finding it in many ways, including gang membership, self-harming and extremism (Gavrielides 2020). Data on radicalisation and extremism paints a disturbing picture about the link between feelings of alienation, not belonging and radicalisation. Questions have also been raised about whether British-born Muslim women have been drawn into radicalisation as a way of making connections or as a 'desperate search to find a place where [they] belong' (Barnett 2015: 5). One researcher concluded, 'Many of the women I contacted sought affection and praise in the arms of the Isis sisterhood. More than anything else, "Umm Raeesa" craved human connection. She had a deep yearning to belong' (Jaffer 2015: 6).

The poem 'Ballad of the Blade' was written by Somali-British Momtaza Mehri and gives an insight into what attracts young people into gang membership and knife crime. The poem is written from the viewpoint of the knife, a symbol of masculinity. Its chilling start is in a child's bedroom. Mehri interspersed her narrative with the voices of those affected by youth violence (the victims, the bereaved families) and those caught up in it (the perpetrators, the gang members). A gang member tells his story about what had drawn him into the gang. It was the search for belonging: 'I found belongingness and a family and affection. I was being lifted up. I was getting all these things I wasn't getting from society. Society was bringing me down saying "you're a black boy, you're a thug". It was always looking down on me' (Mehri 2018).

Experiences that say it all

The walls that divide the world of the school and life in the community are permeable. Ideas, expectations, assumptions seep through. Feelings of dislocation and uncertainty can leak into the lives of young people (John 2011), affecting their sense of identity and contributing to feelings of unhappiness and not belonging. Children from refugee families search for safety – away from those who might wish them physical harm. Some, like Abdi (Vignette 1), find it in that place called school. Others feel outsiders in an alien world which can seem tough, frightening and divided.

In the week following the 2016 referendum about Britain's membership of the European Union, I visited St Anthony's Primary School in South London, a school discussed in Chapter 5. Families come from across the globe. Some are descendants of the Windrush generation or refugees from war-torn areas of the world; others are from long-established families in the community, or have come to the area in search of the respite and opportunities that my family sought in Manchester so many years ago. Following the announcement of the results of the referendum, children had been in tears, asking their teachers, 'Will they send us away?' Their 'place' in the world suddenly felt fragile and uncertain.

This chapter has touched upon the range of factors that contribute to feelings of unhappiness, ostracisation and a sense of not belonging. The pressure to achieve results at any cost, the drive to exclude rather than include, and the experience of being stigmatised (young women facing period poverty) or finding that you don't fit in (children from refugee families) all have damaging and long-term consequences.

The evidence presented reflects the status quo in school systems which take for granted that a significant proportion of young people will fail. This attitude is akin to an educational version of 'planned obsolescence'. As an approach to consumer goods, 'planned obsolescence' sets an artificial limit on the lifetime of a car or washing machine. Transposed to the world of education, it represents a built-in acceptance of failure and exclusion.

Chapter 3 moves away from the impact and consequences of exclusion and a sense of alienation and not belonging in school and offers a more positive narrative. It explores the rich vein of research evidence about the benefits of school belonging, and the relationship between a sense of agency and school belonging.

3
I belong here

> Belonging is about feeling that you have a place, that you matter. If you matter to people, it gives you a sense of who you are. In a school, there only have to be one or two people who know you. It holds you. (Headteacher, quoted in Riley 2017: 63)

Belonging and you

We all bring what we have experienced as children to our lives as adults. Some of the wounds we carry from our past remain raw, and events from our own school days can influence our assumptions about schools today. If our school life was tough and unrelenting, we may be left with a restricted view of what is possible.

Let me invite you to travel back in time to your own school days – your first school, secondary school, high school – whichever comes to mind.

- What did it feel like? Was it a good feeling?
- Did you experience a sense of welcome?
- Were you an insider or an outsider?

Think about your own experience of school life as being governed by a set of traffic lights. *Green* if you had a sense that you belonged and were a part of the school community. *Amber* if you were an 'in betweener' – felt you fitted in sometimes but were on the periphery the rest of the time. *Red* if you experienced a sense of rejection and felt that you didn't belong.

I have used this traffic lights exercise with conference and workshop participants from many parts of the world. Those whose school days enabled them to flow through the green lights become engaged in lively conversations. Understandings are shared, incidents recounted, stories about friends and teachers exchanged. As members of the 'belonging' group bask in the warm glow of happy remembrance, there is a buzz of noise and energy.

Conversations are more muted for those who had hesitated at the amber light. Their discussions are about the vagaries of school life; the circumstances in which they had felt they belonged or were on the outside; what it had meant to be from a family on the move.

> My dad was in the military, we moved school every year or two.
>
> We came from Bangladesh, and we didn't know the rules of the game.
>
> We were the city kids who found ourselves slap bang in the middle of the countryside.

Being different, you stood out. Perhaps you were the newcomer, or the person who did not conform to the conventions of the day: a sporty culture, a girly culture, part of the lads' culture.

For those whose school lives had been brought to a crashing halt by the red light, it was tough to revisit those dispiriting school days. School was a place where you had been bullied or excluded by your peers, ignored or denigrated by your teachers. One participant in this exercise, a teacher, told the rest of her group:

> We were from the other side of the tracks, everybody looked down on us. It was awful. I could make myself sick at 8 o'clock every day so that I didn't have to go to school. That's why I became a teacher. I didn't want anyone else to feel like that.

I included this school belonging exercise as part of a keynote address to the International Congress for School Effectiveness and Improvement in Morocco in 2020: see Appendix 3. It captured the imagination of the 700 plus delegates – policymakers, school leaders, system leaders, researchers, practitioners, master's and doctoral students – from more than 70 countries. At the round-up session, a delegate from a conflict zone in Africa told us about his experience of school life as a refugee.

> I was in a refugee camp. Conditions were desperate but there was a school. Each day my parents would ask me, 'How was school today?' School was the only positive thing in our life in the camp. It wasn't great but we need to remember how important even the most basic school can be for children.

Young people's sense of belonging in school is shaped by what they bring to it: their histories and their day-to-day lived realities, as well as schools' practices and expectations. Our 'traffic light' experiences stay with us, deeply embedded in our psyche and our memories. We remember how we felt in school: all go with the green; a definite stop with the red; waiting around for the amber light to change. Being in touch with our own experiences reminds us of the importance of being part of a place and feeling we belong, in a world in flux.

Schools matter

Schools' policies and practices enable or constrain young people's sense of possibilities, as a seminal piece of research led by Michael Rutter, 'Fifteen Thousand Hours', concluded many years ago (Rutter et al. 1979). Fifteen thousand represented the number of hours young people were expected to be in compulsory education. The study focused on 14-year-olds, examining whether schools' policies and practices had an impact on a range of educational outcomes.

Michael Rutter and his team came up with convincing evidence that some schools were demonstrably better than others at fostering the educational success of their students on such measures as academic achievement, delinquency and attendance. Schools with the best outcomes had high expectations and good teacher–pupil relationships, both in and outside the classroom. These schools had succeeded in creating 'a particular ethos: a positive view of young people and of learning' in schools in which students were given responsibilities, and behaviour management systems were based on inclusive models (Rutter et al. 1979: 88).

'Fifteen Thousand Hours' had a profound influence on me as a young teacher. Its upbeat conclusion that schools in disadvantaged areas could be a force for good underlined the importance of being an inner-city teacher. The study was ground-breaking. It signposted the territory: the importance of positive student–teacher relationships in schools where both staff and young people experienced a sense of possibilities and opportunities. The impact of the research was particularly powerful as I was a newly appointed teacher in one of the 12 schools in the study and a participant in the research, interviewed about my own teaching practices and observed by Peter Mortimore, who subsequently become director of research for the Inner London Education Authority and director of the Institute of Education, London.

Three messages have stayed with me from that study. The first is about the importance of relationships between staff and pupils and expectations. The second is about attendance and the consequences for children's cognitive development if they do not attend school. Young people are unlikely to want to attend a place in which they feel they do not belong and requiring them to 'exit' school, by way of excluding them, reduces their opportunities to make their way through life with hope and in harmony. The third issue is about the strong relationship between the style of leadership and the overall effectiveness of the school, an issue discussed in Part 3. The 'effective' leaders of the Rutter study were strategic and collaborative. Their decision-making was based on a shared vision of what was possible, and their practices drew on the strength of meaningful partnerships with families and communities, a finding echoed in *School Matters* – a study of 2,000 pupils in 50 London primary schools (Mortimore et al. 1988).

Schools as places of belonging

The notion of the school as a potential site of belonging and the language of belonging is a feature of the last two decades. The topic has been explored from a range of disciplines and perspectives and a wealth of evidence has emerged. An early and significant study on the importance of school belonging was carried out by Xin Ma and was based on the experiences of some 14,000 Canadian Grade 6 and 8 students (Ma 2003).

Ma came to define a sense of belonging as the degree to which students felt 'personally accepted, respected, included and supported in the school environment' (Ma 2003: 343). An OECD review of the same period came to a similar conclusion, describing belonging as that sense of feeling accepted at school, as opposed to feeling lonely or rejected (Willms 2003). Drawing on his research findings, Ma concluded that a student's sense of belonging 'was affected more by [their] mental and physical conditions and less by their individual and family characteristics and . . . by school climate characteristics rather than school context' (Ma 2003: 349). The broad conclusions from Ma's research resonate with those of Michael Rutter (Rutter et al. 1979): whatever the social context in which a school is located, what makes the difference is the quality of the daily experience, the relationships and the interactions.

Over recent years, attention has focused on identifying the elements which influence a sense of school belonging. In an overview written for this book, leading Australian academic Kelly-Ann Allen offers a summary of key research data about the importance of school belonging, highlighting the psychological, health and sociological benefits, as well as the long-term consequences of experiencing a sense of not belonging.

The importance of school belonging – by Kelly-Ann Allen

For children and adolescents – facing developmental periods that shape social identity, psychosocial adjustment and transitions into adulthood – the quest to belong at school, where they spend a large proportion of their time, can become a defining feature of their lived experience and an instrumental component of their school success. Our understanding of the benefits of school belonging for students draws from an immense pool of compelling empirical work.

This work demonstrates that a student's sense of belonging to school is a rich and substantial protective factor against mental health problems such as stress, depression and anxiety (McMahon et al. 2008; Moody and Bearman 2004; Shochet et al. 2007; Allen et al. 2018; Allen et al. 2017). In fact, belonging has been identified as the largest known correlate with depression in adolescence (Parr et al. 2020). We also see benefits related to healthy psychological functioning, including psychological wellbeing (Allen et al. 2018; Arslan et al. 2020; Allen et al. 2019), self-efficacy, self-concept, sociability, prosocial behaviour and academic achievement (Abdollahi et al. 2020; Connell and Wellborn 1991; Sirin and Rogers-Sirin 2004; Allen et al. 2017, 2018; Allen and Kern 2017, 2019).

Addressing a sense of school belonging has been found to close the achievement gap by between 50 and 60 per cent (Gehlbach et al. 2016). It also appears that the benefits stretch well into adulthood. Steiner and colleagues from the Centers for Disease Control and Prevention found that school belonging in adolescence had a protective effect in adulthood. That is, adults who felt connected to their school 13 years earlier had reduced emotional distress, physical violence (both as a perpetrator and a victim), use of prescription drug and other drug misuse, and STI diagnosis (Steiner et al. 2019).

We also know that a lack of belonging to school can have an ill effect on wellbeing, prosocial behaviour and, consequently, school outcomes. Poor school social networks have been found to be a predictive factor for suicide ideation and attempts (Wyman et al. 2019). School belonging is also associated with incidents of fighting, bullying and vandalism (Wilson and Elliott 2003), disruptive behaviour, emotional distress (Lonczak et al. 2002), youth radicalisation and school violence (Van Ryzin et al. 2009; Henrich et al. 2005; Roffey and Boyle 2018; Wike and Fraser 2009), smoking, substance use, poor school attendance (Demanet and Van Houtte 2012), and early sexual behaviour (Samdal et al. 1998). School belonging is detrimental to successful school outcomes, and given the innate and fundamental need that belonging plays in the life of most human beings on earth, it stands to reason that for students at school, their sense of belonging plays a critical role (O'Brien and Bowles 2013; Allen 2020).

With colleagues, Kelly-Ann Allen has carried out a meta-analysis on school belonging which provides a rich source of information (Allen et al. 2018). The analysis drew on 51 quantitative empirical studies conducted in Australia, the UK, New Zealand and the United States, undertaken in secondary school settings with young people aged between 12 and 18. Ten factors were identified as influencing school belonging, and the review team concluded that two were of particular importance: student–teacher relationships and positive student attitudes.

Student–teacher relationships had an impact on academic outcomes and on whether young people felt a sense of belonging to their school community. The *student attitudes* which mattered most included having a sense of self-efficacy, a belief in self, coupled with a conscientious approach to their work, and the skills to cope. Researchers have reported that schools which recognise the importance of these two factors have focused on developing the self-reliance and problem-solving skills of young people and strengthening student–teacher relationships (Zimmer-Gembeck et al. 2006).

Within the growing body of literature around school belonging, there is broad agreement that the school environment and schools' practices and expectations influence young people's sense of belonging (Bryk and Thum 1989; Johnson, Crosnoe and Elder 2001; Riley and Rustique-Forrester 2002; Ma 2003; Riley 2017; Allen and Kern 2017). A sense of school belonging has been shown to have a strong association with a range of positive social outcomes, such as health and wellbeing (Putnam 2000). Evidence about the relationship between a sense of belonging and student outcomes can be found in research findings from many countries and contexts and has been linked to student motivation, absenteeism, and academic outcomes (Dunleavy and Burke 2019; Goodenow 1993; Goodenow and Grady 1993; Louis, Smylie and Murphy 2016; Sánchez, Colón and Esparza 2005).

Research which drew on a four-year longitudinal study of more than 500 young people in a Minnesota high school concluded that school belonging was positively associated with a higher level of academic motivation for a student body with Latin American, Asian and European backgrounds (Gillen-O'Neel and Fuligni 2013). A sense of school belonging has also been found to have a positive impact on a wide range of young people, including adolescent females with autism in mainstream schools (Myles, Boyle and Richards 2019).

Evidence from TIMSS (Trends in International Mathematics and Science Study), which is a series of international assessments of the mathematics and science knowledge of students from many parts of the world, shows a significant link between children's sense of physical and emotional 'safety' in school – a key aspect of belonging – and their academic performance in maths and science (IEA 2019). The TIMSS data also reveals gender and country-related differences. Girls are more likely than boys to feel safe in school, and the relationship between a sense of safety and academic performance is stronger for girls than boys. For example, Grade 8 boys (14–15-year-olds) who felt safe in school outperformed their male peers in mathematics and science by 11 points, while girls who felt safe outperformed their female peers by 14 points. Country differences indicate that in Morocco, the strength of the relationship between a sense of safety and performance is particularly high. Grade 4 boys (9–10-year-olds) who feel safe in school outperform their male peers by 25 points and girls their female peers by 27 points (IEA 2019).

Agency and belonging

This chapter closes with an exploration of the relationships between agency and belonging and draws on the research 'School: A Place Where I Belong?' (Study 5, Appendix 1; Riley 2017) to illustrate the ways in which involving young people and staff – and researching for, and about, school belonging – helps develop their sense of agency and belonging. Agency is a concept well developed in the literature and is discussed further in Chapter 6. For Anthony Giddens, agency was about purpose, knowledge, and competence: an ability to 'intervene in the world' to 'make a difference' (Giddens 1984: 14).

The concept of teacher agency has also been explored (for example, Pantic 2015), particularly in relation to teachers' sense of professionalism. The notion of student agency, empowered student voice, has also been explored on moral, physiological, social, educational, pragmatic and democratic grounds (Levin 2000; MacBeath, Myers and Demitrou 2001; Pollard et al. 2000; Riley and Docking 2004) and linked to issues about self-efficacy and exclusion (Riley et al. 2006), and children's rights (Osler 2010).

A significant area of my own research has been on student voice, and I have drawn on a range of research methodologies to engage students (see for example, Flutter and Rudduck 2004; Kellet 2010; Murphy and Torre 2015; Riley and Docking 2004), including involving young people as student-researchers. 'School: A Place Where I Belong?' (Study 5, Appendix 1) involved 35 primary and secondary school student-researchers and 36 teacher-researchers (newly qualified teachers) from 13 London schools, all located in challenging urban contexts (Riley 2017). The research aim was to find out more about how a sense of place and belonging is experienced and generated. A collaborative inquiry approach was adopted, based around a shared research question: 'Is this school a place where everyone feels they belong?' Collaborative inquiry is an approach which has been used to foster greater equity (Ainscow, Muijs and West 2006), and to strengthen children's rights (Osler 2010) and their sense of engagement (MacBeath, Myers and Demitrou 2001; Pollard et al. 2000).

The student- and teacher-researchers involved in the study undertook a range of data gathering activities, including a range of surveys, drawings and interviews. For the student-researchers, school belonging (feeling at home in your own school) was about friendship, involvement, happiness, kindness and mutual respect. It was a vital ingredient of effective learning, as one student-researcher told us: 'If belonging makes you feel more confident, and confidence makes you a better learner, students need to feel like they belong in school to learn most effectively' (Riley 2017: 27).

For the student-researchers, safety – both physical and emotional – was a key aspect of belonging. The interactive nature of belonging was manifested through teamwork, togetherness and mutual respect. The word cloud shown in Figure 3.1 represents the perceptions of students from one of the participating schools about the key aspects of belonging.

One primary school team of student-researchers worked with some 30 younger children aged 5–6 in their own school, using a drawing exercise to understand more about how they experienced school life. Figure 3.2 is an example of one of the drawings. The student-researchers chronicled their research findings in their own individual research journals, discussed these as a team and made recommendations to the school.

Eleven-year-old Zanali was one of the student-researchers who undertook this research task, detailing her observations about the drawing in Figure 3.2 in her own research log. Her careful observations focused on the impact of rejection on the child who had drawn the picture:

Figure 3.1 Belonging is about . . . (how pupils see it). Source: author.

Figure 3.2 Me in the playground (London, England). Source: author.

> I was thinking that if this little one came in from play time . . . and people have been shouting at her, so she comes into the class, how would she feel? . . . She wouldn't be focusing on her learning, she'll focus on how about if they come and do it to me again, and I don't want to go to school anymore, like that. (Riley 2017: 9)

'School: A Place Where I Belong?' also involved teacher-researchers, all of whom were in their first year of teaching. Their focus was on the children in their own classrooms. As teacher-researchers, they asked:

- Who are the outsiders in my classroom?
- How do I get the outsiders to feel that they belong?
- Does a child's sense of belonging in the classroom affect their ability to learn and thrive?

Newly qualified teacher Trisha used a drawing exercise to find out how the children in her classroom felt about their school life. Figure 3.3 is an example of this, showing the unhappiness of this child in many aspects

Figure 3.3 I am sad. Source: author.

of her school life – in the classroom and at lunch time, for example. She tracked the progress of the five children who seemed to be particularly unhappy, concluding from the evidence that they felt alone and isolated, particularly at play time. Trisha's response to her research findings was to work with the children and other staff to develop more inclusive experiences in the playground and classroom.

In Vignette 4, teacher-researcher Matthew describes his research journey, explaining why his research about the experiences of children in his classroom had led him to introduce graphic novels.

Vignette 4: Belonging and the graphic novel: a teacher's story

As a trainee teacher, in fact at any point in your teaching career, there are so many things for you to think about that take your time, energy and focus. You get so bogged down and so involved in the marking – which is important – as well as planning for lessons and thinking about displays. But one thing you should never forget, one of the most important things as a teacher is to think 'What are the needs for every child in my classroom?' I was a member of the NQT group invited to become part of the project on belonging. We were encouraged to think about whether the children in our class felt they belonged and to use our research to find out who were the insiders and outsiders. We learned about different ways of doing this. I started with interviews with the children in my class. I had a lot of children from different backgrounds, and different parts of the world, who didn't have a strong grasp of the English language, and a lot who were displaying traits of dyslexia.

I found that some of the children were disheartened about our reading time, not only the boys but the girls too. For example, I had a child from Lithuania who could read very well in her own language, but because she couldn't speak very much English, we couldn't give her literature appropriate to her level.

So I began to think, what can I do to meet these children's needs? Eventually I stumbled upon graphic novels. I found that the reduced text allowed children to approach a more difficult and complex story. If they couldn't read every single word, they could look at the pictures and this could help them follow the storyline. Using the graphic novels allowed me to have mixed-ability reading groups, enabling the children to learn from each other and explain difficult concepts to each other.

I introduced some Japanese novels – and these read from left to right. It gave them a broad new cultural experience as well, and they became interested in literature from other parts of the world. It had this fantastic effect for these children. They began to investigate books and literature that weren't just within the traditional cultural context that they understood. *It really created a sense of belonging for them, a real buzz, that they got to read those books*. I interviewed the children again. They absolutely loved it all, it had a great effect.

As a teacher and adult, you can't look through the eyes of a child, but research allows you to understand exactly what is going on for them, and what they've been thinking. Research allows you to ask children some questions you probably haven't thought about, and that throws so much light on their feelings. That's the great thing about research and making it very objective. (Adapted from Riley 2017: 83–4)

Drawing on the findings from their research, the teacher-researchers went on to adopt a range of strategies, such as reshaping the spaces within the playground and how they are used; introducing more inclusive and collaborative ways for children to work with each other; developing more opportunities for children to take greater responsibility for their own learning; and expanding the range of pedagogical models used in the classroom.

For fledgling teachers Matthew and Trisha, engagement in the research process had contributed to the development of their sense of professional agency. They had come to recognise that they were part of a place, and that through their actions (their agency), they could shape the nature of how that place was experienced by others: actions that contribute to the development of a positive school climate.

Involvement in the research process developed the reflective and analytical skills of all of the student-researcher groups, helping build their confidence, agency and sense of belonging. For the teacher-researchers, being part of the research process developed their sense of professional agency, enabling them to see the children and young people for who they are.

For both the teacher and student-researchers involved in 'School: A Place Where I Belong?', engaging in a process of purposeful collaborative inquiry enabled them to understand more about the importance and impact of school belonging. In doing this, they also came to recognise their own agency and the ways in which they could help shape school belonging for themselves and others. Chapter 4 illustrates how involvement in the research also helped strengthen community connections for student-researchers.

Part 2
The practice of school belonging

4
Community engagement

> For many of our children home and community are not fixed. Their families might have had status in their home community but are at the bottom rung of the ladder in the UK or appealing against deportations. This raises identity issues because belonging is about the meaning we attach to a place, and our relationship to a place, and the way that this changes. School is about negotiating a new way of belonging. (Headteacher Ruth Docking, quoted in Riley 2017: 12)

The evidence about school belonging presented in the previous chapter throws a powerful light on the relationship between a positive sense of belonging and young people's motivation, happiness, academic achievement and sense of personal agency. This chapter explores the significance of the connections between schools and communities in creating belonging, and the degree to which schools which are successful in creating a sense of school belonging are closely attuned to local realities and engage with young people and their families in a process of creating community and building school belonging.

My place is here

Communities count. What matters to young people is whether they feel they have a 'place' within their community. Tower Hamlets is an inner-city, relatively deprived borough in London's East End. The borough was one of the sites for the study 'Leadership of Place', which used two drawing exercises to explore young people's views about life in school and life in the local community. The school-related prompt was 'What's it like being here in this school?' (good and bad), and the community-related prompt was 'What's it like living around here?' (good and bad) (Riley 2013a).

Figure 4.1, drawn by a young woman from 'Towerhill' secondary school, is one typical illustration from the community-related drawing exercise. The drawing gives a sense of the ways in which she saw her life on the streets as offering starkly contrasting experiences and realities. The left-hand side represents the richness of life in a vibrant multicultural community, while the right-hand side is the downside – the unexpected threats and incidents which can be encountered on the street (Riley 2013a).

In the collaborative research inquiry 'School: A Place Where I Belong?' (discussed in the previous chapter), two of the five student-researcher teams also came from schools in Tower Hamlets (Riley 2017). One of those schools was Towerhill. The Towerhill team began their exploration of school belonging by focusing on their local community. What had brought different groups to Tower Hamlets over the decades? How did they, as young Bengali women, 'fit in' to the broader history of the neighbourhood?

The first Bengalis to arrive in Tower Hamlets were lascars, sailors who worked for the East India Company. The East India docks were in the Isle of Dogs, Tower Hamlets, and the sailors began to settle in Tower Hamlets in the 1920s. Today, Tower Hamlets has the largest concentration of Bengalis in the UK.

Figure 4.1 Life on the streets of Tower Hamlets (London, England). Source: author.

In the extract which follows, student-researcher Nusrat explains what she had learned from her research inquiries in the project 'School: A Place Where I Belong?' and how this had shaped her views about her own sense of belonging, both in the neighbourhood and in her school:

> I began with my local community because my research team felt that this was the place where we belonged: Tower Hamlets and the East End is our 'place'. Through researching the history of my community, I learned about how diverse it has been throughout the years – the Jamme Masjid Mosque on Brick Lane, which was formerly the Machzike Hadath Synagogue for the Brick Lane Jewish community and before that a chapel for London's Huguenot community, is proof of this great cultural diversity.
>
> This has been a place for Christian, Jewish and Muslim communities, making it easier for later groups of immigrants to settle in the area and to achieve a sense of belonging. We can see this in our own close-knit Bengali community. We can see how our families have become part of this place.
>
> This helped us think about our place in school. We thought carefully about place and belonging and what this meant in our school. We discussed how important it is to feel like you belong in school and whether the other students felt like us, that we belonged. We decided that it was crucial to feel at home in your school and in your neighbourhood. (Adapted from Riley 2017: 98–9)

Making links and connections is an important part of developing a sense of belonging. Across the River Thames from Tower Hamlets, the student-researchers' team from a Greenwich school also decided to use their involvement in 'School: A Place Where I Belong?' to explore their own contexts and realities. The team were all recent arrivals to the UK, bringing with them a wealth of experiences and a range of languages. They chose to adapt the research question, 'Is our school a place where everyone feels that they belong?', to 'How good is our school at welcoming newcomers?'

Drawing on their research findings, they worked with staff to develop the school's policy on welcoming new students, translating the linked booklet into 10 languages. The senses of agency which grew from this – their realisation that they could influence their school and had the skills to do this – encouraged them to step beyond the school gate, where they became student-researcher advocates, training other young people across the UK to be researchers.

Having a fixed place that communities can point to and say 'here is my place' is as important for young people as adults. The two examples discussed here from the research 'School: A Place Where I Belong?' (Riley 2017) remind us of the role schools can play in encouraging both first- and second-generation arrivals to define their place in the neighbourhood, in ways that can strengthen their sense of school belonging.

The process of research inquiry which Nusrat and her classmates undertook in Tower Hamlets reinforced their collective sense of belonging – in the school and the community. By researching their community, they discovered their place within it and their place in their school. For the Greenwich student-researchers, engagement in the research inquiry had given a group of young people from many parts of the globe a sense of place and community – and belonging. You can 'meet' the student-researchers from Tower Hamlets and Greenwich in the Art of Possibilities videos (www.theartofpossibilities.org.uk).

The headteachers whose schools were involved in 'School: A Place Where I Belong?' recognised the importance of their local communities and their role as leaders in helping strengthen roots and build connections. In the extract which follows, one headteacher describes the importance of the interplay between the school and its local community and how this influenced her decision to bring the school into the research project.

> For our [students] the notion of place and belonging is incredibly important. And even more so in this time when we are all getting a bit exercised about British values and what it means to be part of a community and how we contribute to our community. Working your way through that is quite a complex process. We are trying to help our [students] find their identity. We are trying to find ways which we can relate on a much more meaningful level with communities. Schools become an agent of community, and the community itself becomes an agent of change within the school itself. And the [students] are representative of that community. They are in this research and participating about it. They are not only benefiting themselves. But they are benefiting the school. (Quoted in Riley 2017: 66).

This explanation not only reflects the importance attached by the headteacher to the school–community relationship but also illustrates how leaders can enact their agency in ways that can affirm the importance of belonging within the school and the wider community: an issue which is taken forward in the section that follows. Further examples are offered of how schools in different contexts have worked to anchor themselves in their communities and the benefits of this for all.

Connecting schools and communities

This discussion starts in Chile, with a group of schools deeply rooted in the communities they serve. It then moves to London, providing the example of St Anthony's school to illustrate how community connections are built and a sense of belonging nurtured.

'A positive school climate is difficult to define and measure', Andreas Schleicher, Director for Education and Skills at the OECD, has argued, adding that when you see it, you recognise it (OECD 2019: 47). This was the case for me in Chile in 2015 when – working with colleagues – I had the opportunity to carry out a parallel study to that of 'Leadership of Place' (Study 3, Appendix 1; Riley 2013a).

The focus of our inquiry in Chile was on publicly funded schools serving highly disadvantaged communities (Riley, Montecinos and Ahumada 2016). The schools involved in the research were all performing extremely well on a range of national criteria. School test scores were running against the grain, and despite the many challenges they faced in their lives, the young people were flourishing academically. As researchers, we wanted to know more about why and how this was happening.

We found schools where the determination of the principals to create places of belonging pervaded the atmosphere. These leaders knew the names of everyone in the local community, and in one instance even the dogs too! As principals, they set about trying to understand community realities and to build social capital, doing this through their daily efforts to create connections and alliances. Alberto Fernández worked to build trust and reciprocity with the community and, over the years, the community had put its own shield round the school, protecting it from the street violence in the neighbourhood. He told us, 'There is a drug problem outside of the school but we have never had it inside the school, never, ever. I believe it is because the community loves the school . . . No one throws a stone.'

In a context of zero-hours contracts, parents had to take the working hours on offer, whenever and wherever they came, leaving children at home on their own for many hours. These principals recognised the pressures on families and did not judge them. In the view of Ana Rodriguez, when children feel secure and contained, they can learn, and this is what the school aimed to do: 'If we have children who come from environments that expose them to psychological violence, with parents who curse at them, then the school must offer a different space.'

In all three schools, staff walked and talked the practice of belonging. Children experienced what it meant to belong daily, and consequently felt visible and valued. They told us that what they had to say mattered. Love shone through. Maria Sánchez counselled love: 'What prevails here are our efforts to give them the greatest amount of love possible. Our school is designed to give children the greatest amount of love' (quoted in Riley, Montecinos and Ahumada 2016: 7).

The 'conceptual cocktail' we witnessed in those Chilean schools was intoxicating. The ingredients in the mix – love, belonging, voice and agency – are words rarely uttered by policymakers. Yet that concoction can be just what schools need, particularly those supporting families who may find themselves at the hard edge of society, such as St Anthony's Catholic Primary School on the edge of Bromley in South London.

St Anthony's

St Anthony's is a one-form-entry school, serving a diverse and transnational community made up of a wide range of ethnic groups. Some of the families are refugees, many others are recent arrivals to the UK. The transient nature of the local population, and the socio-economic problems in the locality, provide the backdrop for the school's ambitious aims to create an inclusive and welcoming community.

My partnership with the school sprang from a mutual commitment to finding ways of creating a sense of school belonging. My role was to contribute to the school's growth through a process of creative engagement with staff and young people. Under the umbrella and aspirations of the 'The Art of Possibilities', DancePoet TioMolina and I worked with young people and staff on a range of activities.

Our work included using poetry performance and music with young people, as a way of enabling them to recognise and appreciate their own talents and skills: a process which helps 'grow' belonging. We set up a student-researchers group, our 'knowledge quest team', who took on the task of researching how children at St Anthony's experienced school belonging (Riley 2017: Appendix II). We supported the innovative thinking of school staff and the school's leadership team, encouraging them to be more explicit in the actions they took, and the language they used to nurture school belonging.

The school is housed in an unprepossessing building: no great architectural gems here. Staff have made extensive use of the many 'spaces' around the school, not only to capture the work of pupils but also to display cultural artefacts and share important messages about what it means to belong at St Anthony's.

Over time, the children at St Anthony's have developed a clear sense of belonging. They are not expected to leave their personal identity behind as they reach the school gate and enter a school in which they can encounter 'people like me'. The school has created quiet places for peaceful reflection. A covered stage in the playground has become the venue for creative performances, including the production of the children's legacy video about school belonging in which they showed how – by intervening to help create a sense of inclusion for all – pupils can exert their agency in the playground.

The beating heart of the school is embedded in the communications and the relationships and held in trust by the transforming nature of the leadership. Belonging is manifested in a determination to create a strong bond between the school and the community. Vignette 5 provides an example of how the school has gone about this.

Vignette 5: Bringing families into the belonging circle – St Anthony's Catholic Primary School, Bromley

St Anthony's decided to use its International Day celebration to reinforce its connections with local families, and to develop a shared understanding about belonging. As parents arrived for the event, they were met by Year 5 student-researchers ('the knowledge quest team') who asked, 'What does belonging mean to you?'

The student-researchers presented their findings from their own research on school belonging to the packed audience of parents and families. The results from the parent survey were later brought together in a word cloud which was mounted on a plaque in the school.

Year 3 children who had been part of the programme on school belonging performed their own interpretation of the poem 'We Refugees' by Benjamin Zephaniah. The poem includes the memorable line, 'We can all be refugees, all it takes is . . .'

The power of both sets of presentations at the school's International Day, a celebration of cultures, beliefs and experiences – symbolised in food and national dress – brought families and their children together. It helped expand a shared appreciation of community, contributing to the growth of trustful relationships that characterise the interactions between the school and the community. All this is part of the process of creating a shared sense of belonging.

The passion for inclusion and excellence at St Anthony's permeates throughout the school. Staff have developed a deep affection for families and the local community, and an understanding of the many pressures they face. Their ambitions for their pupils are boundless. Their commitment to the school is profound and personal. Nothing will stop them – or their pupils.

On 28 December 2021, the young rapper 'Leo', who led the group performance of 'We Refugees', was a finalist in *The Voice Kids*, series 5 (UK), to the delight of will.i.am. The school commented, 'You gave him space to perform.'

The partnership with St Anthony's has taught me that building school belonging takes time, yet the process of engagement reaps many beneficial rewards along the way. A sense of belonging is developed through a purposeful approach in which school leaders learn how to apply their own agency, before developing ways of enacting the agency of others: staff, young people and communities.

In our highly volatile world (Albrow 1996), where new ideas can as easily be built on quicksand as on solid foundations, schools are not only important conduits of information but also among the few shared social institutions which can create a sense of belonging or exclusion.

Headteacher Ruth Docking, whose words introduced this chapter, leads a school in which many of the families find themselves on the margins of society. Her reflections encapsulate the enormity of the challenges and the importance of school for these young people who face major challenges in their life. 'School', she argued, 'is about negotiating a new way of belonging.'

5
Schools where belonging works

> In this school I feel that I belong . . . I can be myself here. I have a personal life and a professional life, and I can make a difference. (Janet Bates, teacher, quoted in Riley, Coates and Allen 2020: 10)

This chapter draws on research on school belonging, carried out in 2020, to highlight the characteristics of schools where belonging works. Belonging cannot be mandated. A sense of school belonging emerges when relationships are nourished in climates of shared expectations and mutual trust. Enabling the micro-climate of belonging to take root, grow and flourish is the art of possibilities. Students appreciate a 'school environment where bullying is unusual, where students do not feel out of place, and where establishing genuine and respectful relationships with teachers is the norm' (OECD 2019: 47).

The art of school belonging

'Place and belonging in school: Why it matters today' was commissioned by the National Education Union (NEU). It comprised a literature review (Study 8, Appendix 1; Allen, Riley and Coates 2020) and case studies (Study 7, Appendix 1; Riley, Coates and Allen 2020). The focus of the research was on exploring the relationship between a sense of belonging, behaviour and learning with the aim of identifying what *was* working, rather than what *wasn't*. What could make a positive difference for young people their families and school communities? The case studies took place in five schools across England: Birdvale, a primary school in the Midlands; Greenvale, a community college in the Southwest; Metroland, a London primary school; Redvil, a primary in the Northeast of England; and Seascape, a primary school in a coastal part of the Northwest.

The literature review had highlighted the strong relationship between good behaviour, the quality of teacher relationships with students, strategies aimed at enhancing the social and emotional aspects of learning, and a sense of belonging. It had revealed little compelling evidence to support so-called 'zero tolerance' policies, sanction-driven approaches to behaviour management (Allen, Riley and Coates 2020). We drew on the findings from the literature review to expand our understanding of the connections between belonging, behaviour and inclusion in school, and to shape the fieldwork activities for the case studies.

In framing the case studies, our aim was to explore the experience and practice of school belonging:

- Did young people and staff feel that they belonged?
- What behaviour policies were in place and what did staff and students think about these?
- How did staff and students talk about learning?
- What actions did the leaders take to create a sense of belonging?
- How did the schools connect to families and communities?

Max Coates and I used a wide range of networks to identify potential case-study schools and to ensure a geographical spread across England, before choosing six (four primary and two secondary) from a longlist of 15 schools, all serving a range of communities facing significant challenges. In making this final selection, we looked for intentional whole-school practices, as well as evidence that the school was on an upward trajectory.

The research began in 2019 and came to a halt in early 2020, as the Covid-19 pandemic took over and day-to-day life as we knew it came to a standstill. Sadly, we missed out on the fieldwork in one of the secondary schools because of Covid. We interviewed the headteachers from the five remaining schools and worked with 49 teachers and teaching assistants and 79 children and young people, in group sessions: a total of 133 young people and adults. The findings from this research have much to offer about the practice of school belonging, the characteristics of schools where belonging works, and the actions which pupils, staff and school leaders can take to make the difference.

The five schools had all faced major issues about behaviour in the past, and recalibrating the school culture had been a challenging undertaking. While each had responded to these challenges in context-specific ways, we found a common aspirational language, as well as expectations and practices which were broadly in alignment with the findings from the literature review.

There was little in these schools about 'tough' sanction-based behaviour policies which depended on exclusion and social isolation. Interventions were characterised by relational approaches which valued individuals. Behaviour policies were owned by everyone. Staff and pupils knew what they were, had helped shape them, and thought they were fair. Exclusions were rare and the responses to students' challenging behaviour were typically, 'Why did you do that?', 'How do you feel?,' 'How do you think other children, or your teacher feel?' or 'What do you think we should do?' As the discussion which follows illustrates, what matters in these schools are communities, teachers, learning, young people and joy.

Communities matter

The schools involved in this research inquiry tailored the practice of school belonging to the local context and community needs. Birdvale is in the middle of a 1930s social housing estate in the Midlands, in a neighbourhood of high disadvantage which has become a first location for many migrant families. It has a significant mix of different cultures, including from Eastern Europe and Africa, and many new arrivals do not have an immediate proficiency in English. The school is dedicated to bringing together more than 800 pupils who between them speak 44 different languages. Name calling, ignoring others, using unkind words, shouting or fighting are out. Being respectful, showing kindness and generosity, taking responsibility for your own learning are what matters.

The leaders of all five schools recognised the importance of contextual and community-oriented approaches, seeing an important part of their role as connecting to parents and responding to community realities. Seascape in the Northwest of England is an example of this.

The school is set in a once-thriving fishing port which, over several decades, has lost its deep-sea fishing role, its ferry service to the Isle of Man and Ireland, and its freight rail link. Over the years, the town has been stripped of its economy and identity. Poverty is endemic, with one in three children living below the poverty line. The practice of school belonging at Seascape is reflected in the steps the school has taken to help rebuild a sense of local identity and boost the self-belief of pupils and parents. The school calls this approach 'Dare to dream': see Vignette 6.

Vignette 6: Dare to dream: Seascape School, Northwest England

In December 2020, when schools were struggling to cope with the impact of the Covid-19 pandemic, details of a school's nativity play hit the headlines. Members of the cast included three socially distanced wise men dressed as Elvis, Mary riding on a Blackpool donkey, and a celebrity cast from a range of TV shows, including *Britain's Got Talent*. The school was Seascape, a school we had visited in early 2020 for this research, just before the first major lockdown for the Covid-19 pandemic. Their 2020 nativity play encapsulated what the school had described to us as its 'dare to dream' approach to school life: a response to the low self-esteem of many families and pupils in the area.

'Dare to dream' was devised as the antidote to low expectations, poor results and a lack of self-belief within the community. It was about envisioning the 'impossible' – dreams and possibilities – and making it happen: skydiving; achieving a Christmas number one song; winning *Britain's Got Talent*. Headteacher Mike Glazier saw his role as showcasing the forgotten children and changing their beliefs about what is possible. The sky is the limit. 'We encourage our pupils to be resourceful, to keep asking [and be] cheeky but polite', he told us.

The staff we interviewed are on board with this aspiration. They have a strong sense of connection to the school and feel that they belong and are valued: 'part of the place'. They are committed to translating the children's dreams into realities. The children found it hard to recall any place or incident within the school where they felt they did not belong.

Within school, the emphasis is on what children can do, not on what they are not allowed to do. Learning is at the centre of school life at Seascape, with intentional approaches aimed at moving learning forward, such as strategies for tackling delayed speech and language, supporting families or changing behaviour. Staff model the behaviour expected of everyone by the ways they work together and show their respect each other. The senior leadership team share an office which is located in a central area of the school. The office is a thoroughfare for staff and children alike and is also the place where Mabel, the school dog, sleeps. She is a friend to all.

The school is a joyous place to be. The children are engaged. Results are rising and numbers are growing. As part of its 'dare to dream' approach to life, the school took a shot at the number one

Christmas single; staged a prequel of the Harry and Meghan royal wedding; and made it to the TV show *Britain's Got Talent*. They did not win but they – and their headteacher – performed spectacularly.

Teachers matter

Research tells us that the most significant factor for young people – in terms of whether they experience a sense of belonging or exclusion in school – is how they perceive their relationships with their teachers (Allen et al. 2018). Teachers are the key influencers for children. How staff feel will affect their relationship with their pupils.

Discussions with staff revolved around two themes: their views about the importance of school belonging for young people; and their own experiences of belonging. Staff emphasised the importance for young people of being part of friendship groups, not cliques. They argued that young people need a wide range of opportunities to define their own success beyond the traditional academic routes, including areas such as drama, music and art.

The staff recognised the strong link between belonging and behaviour. Figure 5.1 represents one teacher's views about the importance of the link between the two. Young people feel a sense of belonging, she suggests, when they have the opportunity to articulate their views, and the space to develop confidence in themselves. Anger, however, is frequently a response to exclusion and alienation: a reflection of that sense of not belonging. Anger could tip a young person over the edge, putting them in conflict with the school, as it did for Kushtrim, whom we met in Chapter 2.

In the second part of our discussions with staff we focused on their own feelings and experiences about school belonging, using a card-sort exercise with statements about belonging derived from research as a prompt (see Appendix 2). The staff we met told us that they felt respected and accepted in school cultures which valued them as individuals and appreciated them as professionals. When you feel you belong . . .

- You can be more creative, innovative and confident.
- You feel respected and accepted.
- You will choose to stay longer in your school because you can make more of a sustained contribution.
- You have a sense of wellbeing and agency: you know that you can make a difference.
- You feel more involved in the life of the school and committed to your job.

Figure 5.1 Belonging and not belonging – a teacher's view.
Source: author.

In these schools, there are few problems about staff retention. Teachers stay. A teacher from Metroland summed it up as follows: 'You commit and know you have a future and that encourages you to be yourself and to innovate.' Knowing that they can make a difference, these teachers have a strong sense of personal and professional agency and commitment to their school. As we began the card-sort exercise about belonging in Redvil, teacher Janet Bates interjected:

> I feel really emotional when I think about this. In this school I feel that I belong. My opinion is heard. I can even say 'I can't cope'. But in my last school, I wasn't trusted. The head was a bit of a bully and told me that I hadn't got what it takes to be a teacher and I nearly quit teaching. Then someone told me to apply here . . . I can be myself here. I have a personal life and a professional life, and I can make a difference.

Learning matters

These five schools are all about learning. The spaces around the schools are used to reflect how children and young people learn; to showcase their creativity; and to highlight contemporary issues, such as climate change and social justice. Values matter. Cooperative values are at the heart of school life at Greenvale Community College: self-help, self-responsibility, democracy, equality, equity and solidarity.

Metroland Primary in Islington serves a diverse and geographically mobile neighbourhood which faces significant challenges in a borough which also has many affluent residents. Headteacher Jane Dryden describes the school as being about children's learning and their independence as learners, seeing her role as being the person who connects the learning. Staff and young people share an understanding about what this means in practice and the brightly coloured 'Metroland Wheel' which greets you as you enter the school is a vivid reminder of the importance of learning, and the key elements in the learning process:

> >< *Create* >< *Remember* >< *Understand* >< *Apply* >< *Analyse* >< *Evaluate* ><

Figure 5.2 captures the important features of what is happening in Metroland to help create a climate for independent learners to flourish, in ways that strengthen their sense of belonging.

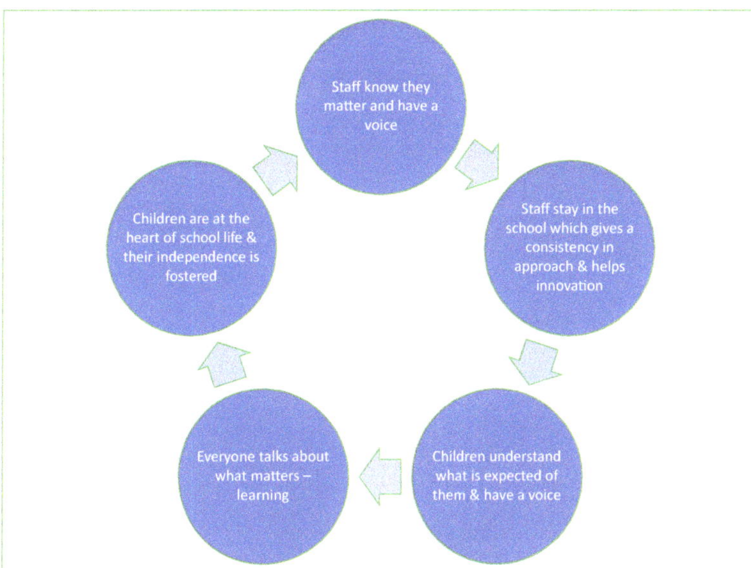

Figure 5.2 Learning and independence, Metroland Primary School, London, England. Source: author.

Figure 5.3 I feel that I belong when I'm learning. Metroland Primary School, London, England. Source: author.

The children from Metroland responded to the drawing exercise by making the connection between a sense of belonging in school and their own learning. They experienced their school as a place of joy and excitement. The drawing in Figure 5.3 is an example of this. Children of all ages in the school love their learning and feel they belong in their classrooms.

Young people matter

As a prompt for the discussion with young people, we used a drawing exercise. We asked, 'What does it look like (in my school) when I feel that I belong? What does it look like (in my school) when I feel that I don't belong?' This exercise revealed a powerful sense of belonging in the 79 children and young people who completed it. In response to our first question, 'What does it look like (in my school) when I feel that I belong?' the images of belonging were invariably warm, frequently glowing and always heartfelt. Children talked about what they liked about being in school and how much they enjoyed the challenges. There was a strong sense that if anything were to go wrong, you could talk to your teacher.

The young people were very clear that there was little bullying, and that it was rare to feel an outsider in their school. They took it for granted that as members of their school community, they had a role to play in bringing other children out of any experiences of isolation, commenting for example that, 'If you don't have anyone to play with in our school, the other children will come up and be your friend.' Their observations mirrored the views of Year 6 students from St Anthony's School about their role in helping create a sense of school belonging: see Appendix 2.

When we asked, 'What does it look like (in my school) when I feel that I don't belong?' both boys and girls recognised that things could go wrong in the ebb and flow of friendship patterns. However, the drawings of exclusion and unhappiness which emerged from this exercise were derived from their sense of empathy about how it *might* feel like to be an outsider, to not belong, to be rejected, rather than as a description of having experienced this: see Figure 5.4.

Figure 5.4 Rejection feels like this. Source: author.

Joy matters

Redvil is located in the Northeast of England in a large 1950s post-war council estate of social housing which today is an area of high unemployment and deprivation. When Dave Phillips held his first parents' meeting as the new headteacher at Redvil, no one came. The empty hall for the parents' meeting was a representation of the gap between the school and the local community. School 'learning' was an alien and joyless experience – as much for parents as for their children.

Over recent years, the school has stepped out into the community in a concerted process of shared involvement. The doors have swung open to families and communities who have long been reluctant to cross the school's threshold. An open and welcoming approach now draws parents into the regular Friday afternoon 'bestseatsinthehouse' assembly which celebrates the many achievements of the children. Families flock in and out of the school with confidence and ease. Children bounce with joy and eager anticipation to hear who has been given the weekly 'Stars of the Week' awards. Figure 5.5 expresses that sense of joy and belonging of being a 'star' as your family and friends cheer you on: see also Vignette 7, Chapter 9.

Achievement takes many forms at Redvil and the children are rewarded by books from a specially adapted vending machine. Practices are intentional, connected and consistent. For the children at Redvil, belonging is about love, respect, being part of a family – and joy.

Making sense of it all

The schools involved in this research share a number of common features. A sense of belonging is manifested in relationships at all levels and can be seen in the ways in which staff and students talk to, and about, each other. Staff and students feel they belong. They are heard and seen for who they are. They have a sense of agency. The schools work to apply intentional, connected and consistent approaches.

- *Intentionality* implies purposeful and positive interventions (not one-off reactions) that are understood across schools and school systems.
- *Connectedness* is about common purpose and ensuring that the actions taken are understood and valued. When 'connectedness' is working, local school systems understand their role in the national framework.

Figure 5.5 'Star of the Week', Redvil Primary School, Northeast England. Source: author.

Within schools, staff, children and young people perceive the school, and what goes on there, as being meaningful and important to them.

- *Consistency* is manifested in the ways in which children and staff speak about what goes on in the same way. There is a mutual understanding of what matters.

Two broad conclusions have emerged from the research reported in this chapter. The first is that pupils who have a sense of belonging in school tend to be happier and more confident and perform better academically. The second is that intentional whole-school practice can help create a climate of welcome and belonging in school. While each of the headteachers of these schools would undoubtedly say that the school they lead is a 'work in progress', the evidence from the research leads to the conclusion that a purposeful approach brings everyone on board, enriches the lives of all concerned and sets the school on a positive and upward trajectory.

The value of building connections and involving parents and families in the school life of their children cannot be underestimated. The actions taken by the schools taking part in this research in building community and connections seem to fit the OECD's view of what is important: 'By encouraging parents to . . . be more aware of their children's interests and concerns, and show interest in their school life . . . [and by] establishing relationships based on trust, schools [can)] rely on parents as valuable partners in the education of their students' (OECD 2019: 49).

6
Tools to take your thinking forward

This short chapter is by way of a staging post, offering a range of conceptual tools and lenses designed to deepen understanding about how school belonging is experienced. These can also be used to identify potential trigger points: the changes in day-to-day practices or the leadership actions which can make a difference, or the policy shifts needed to create a positive climate.

Figure 6.1 presents the chapter's structure and three themes: ways of thinking; ways of understanding; and ways of locating. Sense-making tools or linked concepts are also introduced to illustrate each theme.

Ways of thinking about what goes on in school: the 'Prism of place and belonging'

A sense of belonging is both a highly individual experience and a social construct. The 'Prism of place and belonging' is a conceptual tool which offers a way of scanning the daily realities of school life with a fresh eye and open mind.

A prism refracts the light or breaks it into different parts (see Figure 6.2). As the beam is dispersed, the 'big picture' becomes separated and the different elements within it can be seen. By taking different wavelengths and condensing them into white light, prisms can also do the opposite. This is akin to taking all those aspects of school life which are connected to relationships and emotional encounters – inclusion, exclusion, wellbeing and physical and mental health, cyber-bullying – and bringing those experiences together them in one shared narrative: that of belonging. You might like to think of the prism as a fairground mirror, a looking glass which enables you to see things in a very different way – and just look where it took Alice in her Wonderland!

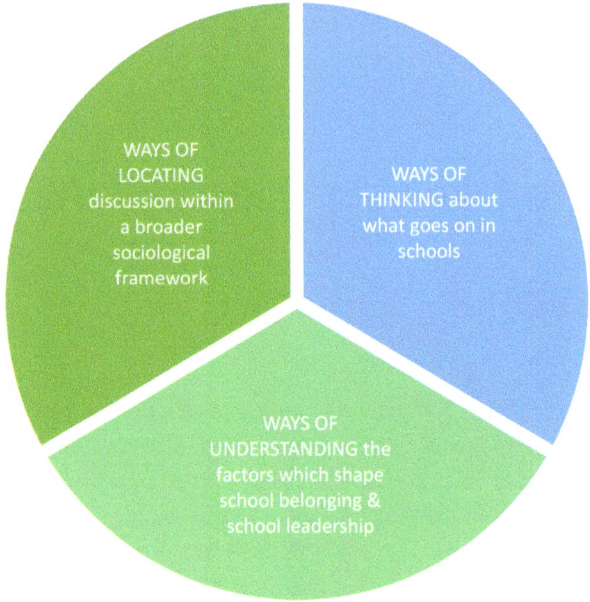

Figure 6.1 Ways of thinking, understanding and locating. Source: author.

Figure 6.2 The 'Prism of place and belonging'. Source: author.

The 'Prism of place and belonging' offers its own a distinctive window into school life, as both a conceptual instrument to frame research and a development tool. As a research instrument, the prism can be used to help think about the main research question, as was the case for 'School: A Place Where I Belong?', which asked the question 'Is this school a place where everyone feels they belong?' (Study 5, Appendix 1; Riley 2017).

As a developmental tool, the prism has been used to help staff distinguish between what they *think* is happening in the school and what they *know* to be happening. Taking account of where the light falls enables staff to make fresh links and connections, and to ask: who are the insiders and who the outsiders in this school? Who feels that they belong and who doesn't? What areas of the school do staff and young people feel most comfortable in – and where are able to be creative and insightful?

Young people's sense of belonging in school is grown or shattered by what they encounter on a daily basis. Some of the drawings already presented in the book, such as Figures 2.1 and 3.2 (pages 33 and 47), illustrate this point. Looking through the 'Prism of place and belonging' becomes a way of acknowledging realities: the first step to developing the actions and approaches which can help build belonging as an intrinsic part of the daily life of a school.

Ways of understanding the factors which shape school belonging and leadership

Belonging: a dynamic concept

The conceptual tool 'Belonging: a dynamic concept' brings together the three sets of factors which shape young people's sense of belonging in school, what I describe as the: outside-in; inside-out; and the leadership walk and talk: see Figure 6.3.

Outside-in is the first part of the framework and represents the connections between school and non-school life. Every person who enters the school gate – be they an adult or a young person – brings with them their own personal histories, experiences, identities and beliefs. These represent their day-to-day lived realities, as well as their past experiences: the weight and joy of the external conditions in which they find themselves; the incidents and contextual circumstances which shape their daily lives in their communities. Schools' practices and expectations come into play even before young people enter the school gates. They are manifested in the ways that schools respond to the complex factors

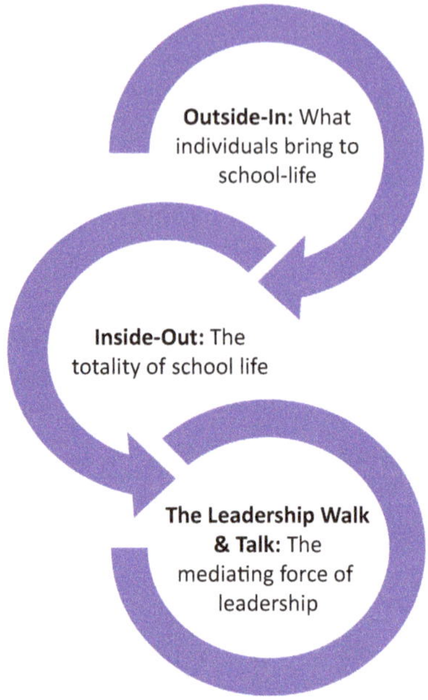

Figure 6.3 Belonging: a dynamic concept. Source: author.

in people's lives and the degree to which some voices are heard, while others are ignored.

Inside-out represents the totality of school life. This is expressed in the school culture and mirrored in the daily practices which contribute to a sense of belonging or exclusion. Relationships are key, particularly student–teacher relationships. The school's implicit or explicit views and beliefs about whose voices count, or who is capable of learning, are evident in myriad actions and inactions by individuals and groups within the school. Words matter: the lexicon of belonging and inclusion versus the language of rejection and exclusion. The school's climate is pervasive, representing a belief in possibilities or an acceptance of defeat. A positive and inclusive climate is manifested in the ways in which:

- teachers talk to each other, about each other, to the children;
- young people are encouraged to interact with, and talk to, their peers and adults;
- school leaders refer to their staff, discuss matters, talk to and about the children and their families.

The climate shapes the environment for learning. It determines whether the spaces around the school are experienced as spaces of safety (physically and emotionally) and creativity, or fear and rejection.

The leadership walk and talk is the third element in the framework and represents the relationship between actions and beliefs. A sense of school belonging is grown or stifled by the mediating force of leadership. How leaders walk their talk sets the tone, the culture and the possibilities (Riley 2013a, 2017). The tenor of the language, the vocabulary of inclusion or 'othering' sets possibilities and boundaries. How school leaders enact their own agency – and endorse the agency of staff, young people and communities – will shape what is possible. As will be discussed later, new forms of compassionate leadership are required in these uncertain times.

Taking the leadership pulse

'Taking the leadership pulse' is a tool for identifying the key elements that influence school leaders' ability to manage and maintain their balance and focus. The tool incorporates the four realities of leadership – the physical; the social and political; the emotional; and the spiritual and ethical.

- The physical reality: This represents how school leaders respond to the speed and complexity of everyday events in the built environment in which staff and students live and work, and all that happens within it.
- The social and political reality: This encapsulates how leaders make sense of, and react to, the social landscape, the community context of the school and the political and policy environment which shape policy and decision-making.
- The emotional reality: The emotional reality of leadership is experienced in the complex interactions which characterise a school day. It is also influenced by the physical, social and political realities, as well as the relationships between individuals and groups in the school.
- The spiritual and ethical reality: The degree to which leaders are attuned to their own beliefs – the moral, spiritual and ethical imperatives that drive them as school leaders – and draw on these to shape their actions has a significant effect on their sense of balance and equilibrium.

'Taking the leadership pulse' was originally created as a development tool but later also proved to be a useful research tool for mapping the realities which school leaders face in different contexts and was subsequently used in research in the US, UK and South Africa (Riley 2013a), Morocco (Elmeski 2013) and Chile (Riley, Montecinos and Ahumada 2016). Embedded within this framework is the notion of leadership as a 'stool' resting on four legs: the four realities. Given the pressures, leaders need to be able to sit comfortably on their leadership stool. If one of the legs is 'wobbly', they will find themselves out of kilter – and might fall off their perch (Study 5, Appendix 1; Riley 2007).

Locating the discussion about belonging within a broader sociological framework

This final theme touches on the concepts which I have drawn on to help me understand more about school belonging. Concepts are abstract ideas which can be used to help make sense of the bigger picture. In this final section of the chapter, I introduce three key concepts – *space*, *social capital* and *agency* – which have helped me locate the discussion about school belonging within a broader sociological framework. Two pieces of research have contributed to my understanding of the relevance of these concepts to school belonging: 'Leadership of Place' (Study 3, Appendix 1; Riley 2013a) and 'School: A Place Where I Belong?' (Study 5, Appendix 1; Riley 2017). The three concepts appear throughout the book.

Space

Space, or the lack of access to space, is a critical issue for young people, particularly those living in an urban environment. Many of today's urban children are transported from one child-specific place to another. This can lead to the development of a process of 'insularisation' in which the spaces within the school assume additional meaning and importance for young people (Kernan 2010). As Sol Perez Martinez has argued, 'the urban child has lost his or her independence and mobility' as a result of a range of issues, including security and traffic (Martinez 2018: 29).

The school is both a physical and an emotional 'space': the 'friendship bench' in the playground which offers a safe haven for children on the margins of school life who struggle not to be an outsider; the hidden spaces at the back of the sports hall which can feel unsafe and uncertain. The 'spaces' each young person or staff member inhabits or passes through have a profound impact on their sense of self, and on their sense of place and belonging. The school is also a liminal space, a place of transition and uncertainty, particularly for new arrivals, and yet also a space which offers the possibility of opportunity and transformation.

The research 'Leadership of Place' (Riley 2013a) also shed light on the ways in which school leaders can chose to exert their 'agency' to create spaces within school where young people can feel safe and confident in who they are. The study provided powerful evidence about the benefits of positive connections and collaborations with communities and led me to recognise the importance of social capital in building school belonging (Study 3, Appendix 1; Riley 2017a).

Social capital

Social capital has been defined as 'networks, together with shared norms, values, and understandings that facilitate cooperation within or among groups' (OECD 2007: 103). Evidence from a range of sources indicates that a focus on social networks and relationships (Bourdieu 1999; Coleman 1988; Putnam 2000) enables educators to look for the positive features of the cultures of newcomers, rather than those that emphasise what they lack (Brunn and Delaney-Barmann 2001).

Within the sphere of education, attention has focused on the educational benefits of building social capital, as a way of creating a sense of social cohesiveness, particularly in communities with large minority or poor populations. This in its turn helps generate a 'sense of place' for children, young people and adults (Elliot et al. 2002; Glasman and Crowson 2001; Helliwell and Putnam 2007; Morris and Morris 2002).

The research 'Leadership of Place' provided evidence about the benefits of harnessing social capital and shone a spotlight on the role of leaders in doing this. School leaders who saw themselves as leaders of place worked to build social capital. They did this by reaching out to communities, building bridges and strengthening networks: an approach which in its turn helps build that intangible asset, mutual trust (Study 3, Appendix 1; Riley 2013a). There is evidence that this approach is being taken up by an increasing number of school leaders (Berg, Melaville and Blank 2006; Dyson and Gallannaugh 2008; Riley 2013b).

Agency

The concept of agency has already been introduced in Chapter 3. The term 'agentic action' has also been used by scholars (Richardson 2015).

As discussed in Chapter 3, one powerful finding from 'School: A Place Where I Belong?' was the degree to which engagement in a process of collaborative inquiry around the question 'Is our school a place where everyone feel they belong? generated a sense of voice, agency and belonging for both student- and teacher-researchers (Riley 2017).

The importance of school leaders' sense of agency is well recognised in the literature (Clarke and Wildy 2011; Lovett, Dempster and Fluckiger 2015), and agency is undoubtedly a key factor in creating the conditions for school belonging. Throughout the book, you will find examples of how school leaders have exercised their agency in purposeful ways.

Part 3
Rethinking leadership for belonging

7
Leading through the labyrinth

> In a global context which . . . is increasingly one of alienation and disengagement, and the possibilities of radicalisation, schools need to offer a safe and secure environment for young people in which they can feel they belong. (Headteacher, quoted in Riley 2017: 65)

Schools can and should be places of welcome, possibility and belonging. Whether a school becomes a place of belonging (as the left-hand side of Figure 7.1 demonstrates), or a closed place where young people are ostracised by a clique, and staff feel unappreciated (the right-hand side of the image), is shaped by the leadership of the school.

This chapter explores leadership in challenging contexts and at difficult times, using the notion of leadership as a place-based activity which draws on the social capital often lying dormant in poor communities to help build agency and a sense of belonging. The chapter also introduces the 'Three Cs Framework' of compassion, connectivity and communication as a scaffolding for thinking about new forms of responsive leadership.

The job of being a school leader has always been a tough but rewarding one, full of challenges and dilemmas (Sergiovanni 1992). Testing times and testing circumstances inevitably produce situations in which beliefs become contested, or trust is put to the test (Bryk and Schneider 2002; Louis 2007). Disconnections can emerge which rattle the moral basis on which leaders ground their leadership (West-Burnham 2015). When global, national or local events spin lives around, school leaders find themselves at the helm, struggling to lead through confusion and disruption, as they encounter some of the harsh realities which impinge on the lives of young people and their communities.

School leaders are the mediating force whose values, actions and inactions shape the conditions for school belonging, or produce a climate

Figure 7.1 What kind of school do I want to lead? (Riley, Mendoza and Gonzales 2020).

of exclusion. Findings from research conducted by the Centre for High Performance illustrate this point (Hill et al. 2017). The research team studied the changes made by more than 400 UK headteachers from the time of their appointment, until they relinquished their leadership. They observed that the rewards – in terms of money and honours from the queen – had been given to a group the researchers designated 'surgeons' (Hill et al. 2017). These were leaders whose absolute focus on test results had led them to exclude one in four final-year students, and to dismiss or move on one in ten staff.

The researchers concluded that the public accolades which had been heaped on the 'surgeons' had been based on short-term results, gained at the expense of the emotional health and wellbeing of students and staff. Belonging was clearly not high on the agenda of these 'surgeons'. However, for leaders of place, it is a central feature of their leadership.

Leadership of place

In the collaborative research and development inquiry 'Leadership on the Front Line', I worked with some 70 headteachers and school principals from primary, secondary and special schools, over a four-year period. The schools were in some of the most disadvantaged localities in the UK, and elsewhere (Riley and Emery 2007; Riley 2008). In the context of the communities they served, how did they walk their leadership?

In order to understand more about place and community, one distinctive element of the methodology used in this research was the introduction of a series of developmental conferences which brought the leaders together to share their experiences of managing complex contextual realities. They served communities facing extremes of poverty and social deprivation, including those divided on sectarian grounds; and yet they were communities whose hidden strengths could be drawn out through school–community partnerships based on mutual respect and understanding.

Drawing on the research, I developed a tool, 'Taking the leadership pulse' (described in Chapter 6), with the aim of identifying the key elements that influence school leaders' ability to manage and maintain their balance and focus. The tool incorporates the four realities of leadership: the physical; the social and political; the emotional; and the spiritual and ethical. Together they form the four legs of the stool that sustains leaders.

One finding from 'Leadership on the Front Line' was that to be secure on their stools, school leaders needed to know themselves as leaders (their strengths and flaws); be finely attuned to the contexts in which they were working and the needs and aspirations of communities; and have a clear understanding of their leadership realities. The study revealed the degree to which school leadership is bound in culture and context, and that knowing and understanding the community is a key aspect of effective leadership (Study 5, Appendix 1; Riley 2007).

In 'Leadership of Place', which followed on from 'Leadership on the Front Line', the focus was on how leaders articulated and enacted their leadership in relation to their local communities (Study 3, Appendix 1; Riley 2013a). This research involved 15 principals of schools located in communities facing a range of socio-economic challenges in Brooklyn, New York; London's East End; and South Africa's Eastern Cape. Some of the contextual findings from this research have already been reported in Chapter 2.

The leaders involved in this research were highly aspirational for the children and young people in their schools and empathetic to the challenges their families faced. Their deep levels of understanding and appreciation of community realities had led them to reach out to communities, build bridges and strengthen networks: an approach which had proved to be highly successful in building trust and harnessing social capital, as the following examples illustrate.

- A Brooklyn school principal invited an ex-gangland leader who had been in a federal prison for 10 years to work with students. 'He had currency with the kids . . . He could talk their language . . . they talked about how to deal with gangs,' she explained (Riley 2013b: 96).
- A school in London's East End, with a largely Muslim population, set up a political forum, a safe social space where students could talk about controversial issues and find their voice. The headteacher reflected, 'Young people have a right to express themselves about how they feel. If you feel as a person that society is against you, your race, your language, or your culture, it creates resentment' (Riley 2013b:117).
- A principal in South Africa's Eastern Cape linked with local communities to ensure that a shabeen – notorious for drugs – was moved from outside the school gates. Motivated by a determination to build skills, confidence and self-reliance, a neighbouring principal helped set up a small handicraft workers' cooperative (Riley 2013b).

These place leaders saw their role as setting expectations, encouraging self-efficacy, and providing opportunities for young people and adults to develop their learning, thinking and practice. They sought to create the spaces within schools where youngsters could feel safe and confident and reach out beyond the school boundaries in ways which might help transform localities into neighbourhoods.

The construction of leadership as a place-based activity – and the notion of 'Leadership of Place' which emerged from this research – implies a leadership theory of action and intent which recognises the interconnections between place, social capital, agency and a sense of belonging (see Figure 7.2). Place and belonging are at the core of the model – the heart of the leadership intention. Agency follows. Leaders who are place leaders recognise their own agency and their role in activating the agency of others. Part of their effectiveness as leaders relates to how responsive they are to their local contexts (Riley and MacBeath 1998).

Developing agency and building social capital are inextricably interlinked by the ways in which place leaders strive to develop young people's sense of self and identity within school and make connections with the other communities young people belong to. The knowledge leaders gain from doing this, enabling them to grow connections and 'curate' the spaces within the school in response to the needs of communities.

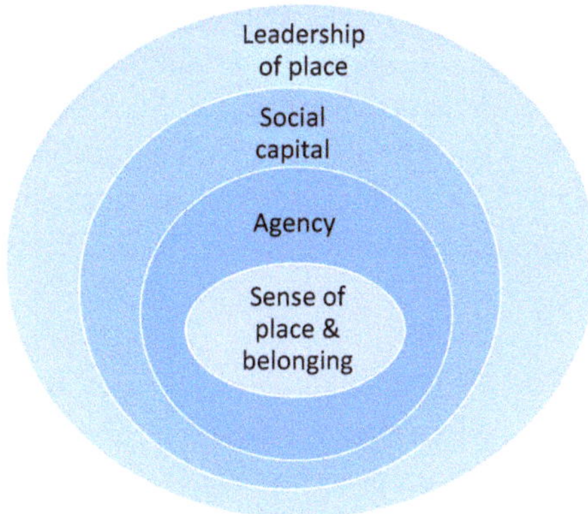

Figure 7.2 Leadership of place: a theory of action and intent.
Source: author.

The notion of leadership as a place-making activity, highly dependent on the agency of school leaders, relies on the willingness and ability of leaders to:

- activate the physical and emotional spaces within the school;
- trigger the agency of staff and students;
- develop vibrant connections with communities, aimed at harvesting the social capital that is all too frequently ignored in disadvantaged communities.

Leading through crisis

When a crisis comes to call, knowing yourself and knowing your community become invaluable leadership assets. At these moments, the importance of schools in the lives of young people also assumes an even greater significance. Three examples are offered to illustrate the impact of unexpected and extreme events on schools and school leaders. Such occurrences add yet another layer to the complexity and nature of what it means to be a leader and reinforce the importance of trustful relationships between schools and communities.

Illustration 1

The unexpected event for London headteacher Nina Blum was an Islamic extremist attack – the very public murder of an off-duty soldier, Lee Rigby, in 2013 – close to the school she led, Corelli School in Woolwich. The student make-up at the time was 35 per cent Muslim, 30 per cent Christian and 10 per cent Buddhist. The attack was captured on social media and shared globally. Its impact on the school was immediate and visceral. One of the assailants turned out to be an ex-pupil. Another ex-pupil was a witness to the murder and comforted the dying soldier. Nina described events in the following terms:

> The thing that all headteachers dread is a crisis in the public domain. The incident was not just one of mindless violence; it was a calculated attempt to create social unrest, and it had the potential to do just that. Much of the press turned it into a vilification of Islam, tarring all Muslims as potentially the same as the murderers. Our values about social responsibility, caring for others, openness and honesty, democracy, are in the bloodstream of staff and students. We've worked on them for many years. We had to support the community in its grief by making sure that we listened to all of the different voices, Lee Rigby's family, members of the Muslim community, staff who had taught the assailant and those who had taught the person who comforted Lee as he died. We had to give our young people the space to talk about how they were feeling and stand together in the face of outside attempts to denigrate one section of the community. (Adapted from Riley 2017: 20–1).

Illustration 2

In May 2017, a suicide bomber targeted a concert in the Manchester Arena. Twenty-three people were killed and 500 injured in an Islamic terrorist attack which rocked the nation. Eighteen thousand people attended the concert to see the American singer and actor Ariana Grande: the majority were girls and young women. The attack touched many lives: the children and staff who went to the concert; those who knew someone who had been there; those who knew someone who never came back. Eight pupils and one teacher from Harrop Fold School in Bolton were present. In the shocked space that followed, headteacher Andrew McVane used a television broadcast to showcase the school as a beacon of belonging which welcomed young people from across the globe, including Rani, from war-torn Syria (Chaudhari 2017).

Illustration 3

In June 2017, a fire broke out at Grenfell Tower, a 24-storey public housing block in London which housed a very diverse population facing many challenges. Seventy-one children and adults died. Six months later, with survivors demanding justice and questioning why residents' concerns about safety had gone unheeded in one of the richest parts of the UK (Kensington and Chelsea), many families were still without permanent homes. Mary Brown, headteacher of Oxford Gardens, a local primary school, also stepped into that public space to talk about the impact of the fire on the school and the local community. 'What happened has changed lives', she commented, 'and we have to work with that, but it's about building something back that is stronger and more resilient' (Rustin 2017). To date, Grenfell Tower remains a burnt-out shell, casting its shadow over the neighbourhood and on the children at Oxford Gardens as they play.

Schools respond to major incidents in different ways. Some ignore them, as was my own experience as a teacher at the time of the New Cross Fire and Brixton Riot (see Chapter 2). This was not the case for the three headteachers whose experiences are described here. They each stepped into the shared space through 'standing together' (Nina), welcoming newcomers from afar (Andrew), and 'building something back that is stronger and more resilient' (Mary). Their responses signalled a deep relationship between the school and the community: a recognition of the 'agency' of the headteacher, both within the school and beyond its formal boundaries, and the importance of schools as places of belonging – and compassion.

The 'Three Cs Framework': Compassion, Connectivity and Communication'

The 'Three Cs Framework' (Figure 7.3) was designed to capture the sense of compassion and drive for connectivity (within and across communities) and ongoing, reciprocal communication which characterised the actions of these three school leaders and other leaders discussed in the book. The point where compassion, connectivity and communication intersect represents the essence of what it means to lead with compassion. The framework draws on research on school belonging (Studies 7 and 8, Appendix 1; Riley, Coates and Allen 2020; Allen, Riley and Coates 2020); a cross-sector collaborative inquiry on the interventions, practices and system-wide changes in policy and practice needed to create school belonging (Study 10, Appendix 1; Riley Mendoza and Gonzales

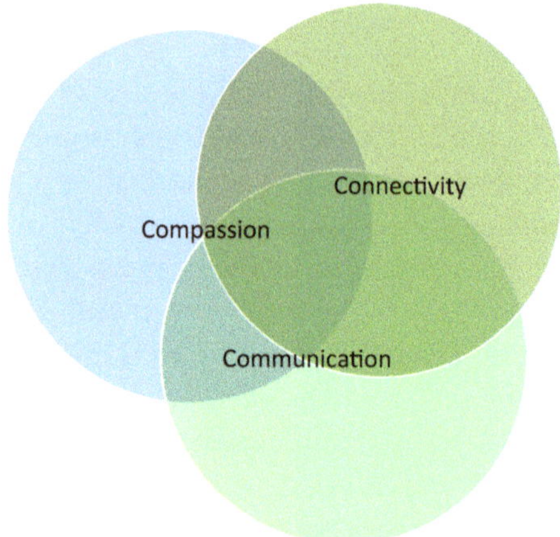

Figure 7.3 The 'Three Cs Framework': Compassion, Connectivity and Communication. Source: author.

2020); and research on leadership during Covid-19 reported in the next chapter (Study 9, Appendix 1; Riley and Mendoza 2020).

Embedded in this framework is the notion of intentionality: purposeful and planned actions put in place by school leaders who assert their agency, and through a relational approach, enact the agency of others, as was illustrated in the research reported in Chapter 6. The headteachers were finely attuned to the needs of the neighbourhood. Their leadership was contextual and community oriented. They were authentic and knew who they were. As one Year 6 child had put it, 'If you're the headteacher, you just have to be who you are.'

Their approach was learning-centred and they understood their own agency and their role in activating the agency of others. These school leaders modelled what they did, monitored what they did, and talked about what they did – all the time, in leadership approaches which were highly relational – with staff, young people and families. They displayed their care and compassion as leaders. The section which follows explores the themes of the 'Three Cs Framework' in more detail.

Compassion, connectivity, communication

Compassion

Researchers have argued that we are hard-wired for compassion and that the journey to kindness and compassion has benefits for all (Gilbert

2013). The notion of compassionate leadership has emerged over recent years in fields dealing with social policy issues, most notably in the healthcare sector, and gained traction during the Covid-19 pandemic, as an effective way of engaging, motivating and supporting staff through extraordinary challenges (Bailey and West 2020). Evidence suggests that compassionate leaders are present and recognise what is important for themselves and their colleagues: see for example, work developed by the Kings Fund (2020).

The concept of compassionate leadership is strongly aligned to that of 'caring leadership', expressed in the work of leading US researchers Mark Smylie, Joe Murphy and Karen Seashore, who argue that caring leaders see their leadership as a community-based activity and use their skills to cultivate caring communities (Smylie, Murphy and Seashore 2020). A review of the literature on positive leadership undertaken to support the research on caring leadership (Seashore and Murphy 2018) indicates that caring leadership contains four orientations:

- a positive orientation (a focus on resources and people);
- a moral orientation (a 'moral imagination' to do the right thing);
- a relationship orientation (a caring and developmental-based attitude); and
- a stewardship orientation (seeing their work as fostering the needs of individuals, groups and the organisation, as well as stakeholders).

Caring leaders set clear boundaries and expectations, apologise for their mistakes and are physically and emotionally present in the lives of people. Their leadership has a significant impact on young people's performance in school, and on their social and emotional learning (Smylie, Murphy and Seashore 2020).

Connectivity

Connectivity is the commitment to collaborate, and the recognition of the importance of making connections and taking steps to ensure that young people feel strongly connected to their school, as Robert Blum (2005) argued. Blum drew on research from the fields of health and education to make a powerful case for 'school connectedness', arguing that this is a key positive factor in young people's experience of school life. He identified three school characteristics as being particularly significant in helping young people to feel connected to school, and in encouraging their sense of achievement: high academic standards and a culture of strong support from teachers; a positive and respectful environment; and a sense of physical and emotional safety.

A sense of school connectedness is the counterweight to experiences of bullying or feelings of social isolation. It reduces the likelihood that young people will engage in 'health-compromising behaviours' (Blum 2005: 1). Connectedness comes not just from policies but from individual actions, and takes place when learning is meaningful and relevant.

Connectivity and collaboration go hand in hand, and the drive to collaborate and connect is a vital attribute in uncertain times. Researchers from many parts of the globe have concluded that leadership approaches which reach out and connect to communities are effective in many ways. They can help remedy inequities and, through a process of engagement, create schools in which adults and young people thrive. These findings hold true for a range of countries and contexts, such as Australia (Gurr et al. 2014) and South Africa (Naicker, Chikoko and Mthiyane 2014).

Communication

Connectivity and collaboration are essential ingredients in building social capital and are linked to communication. In combination, they signal a determination to develop more equitable partnerships with families and communities, as exemplified in findings from UK researchers on school–community partnerships (Ainscow, Muijs and West 2006). Consistency is also a key part of communication, contributing to the development of shared understandings about what is important. School leaders set the tone by how they communicate, who they talk to, and who they listen to. Their communications send messages about what and who matters.

Issues around communication raise many important questions. When leaders communicate with young people, are they asking for their opinions? Are they asking for their opinions about things that matter? Based on her research on the role that student voice can play in school reform in the United States, Dana Mitra has concluded that the most important outcomes of youth participation in student voice initiatives are 'agency, belonging, competence, deliberation and (civic) efficacy' (Mitra 2018: 483).

Questions about the ways in which schools communicate with families and communities are equally important. Is this a two-way process? Are the messages directed at a narrow group of parents who feel comfortable with the school's structures (by dint of language, class or familiarity with school systems) or are they intended to be more wide-ranging and inclusive? Whose voices are heard and valued? When school and community leaders step together into a more equitable and reciprocal space, as Ann Ishimaru has argued, community relationships are transformed by this new dynamic, and recalibrated in a process of equitable collaboration which builds on the social capital in communities (Ishimaru 2018).

8
Leading with compassion

> I feel I belong everywhere around this school. They know that I like it here and they know that I want to be here, and I want to take part in things. (Children from St Anthony's Primary School)

Leading in a pandemic

In a context of mounting uncertainty during the early stages of the Covid-19 pandemic, headteachers found themselves centre stage and the nature of the relationship between the school and the community became even more critical. As school leaders, they had to juggle a multiplicity of roles, while at the same time taking ultimate responsibility in their schools and managing their personal lives. Many were left struggling to catch breath and striving to keep the lid on the pressure cooker.

This chapter draws on data from the inquiry 'Leading in a New Era', undertaken in 2020–1, which involved 16 headteachers in England. The research emerged from a recognition on the part of the three local authorities involved (Telford and Wrekin Council, Hackney Council and Islington Council) of the pressures and demands on school leaders generated by the Covid-19 pandemic, and the important role of local government in supporting them (Study 9, Appendix 1; Riley and Mendoza 2020).

We worked with the headteachers on a locality basis, organising our time together as a personal and professional space for deep thinking and reflection. We mapped their responses to lockdown (how was it for them personally and professionally?); tracked the degree to which their leadership approach altered in response to the Covid-19 pandemic (how did they 'walk' their leadership during lockdown?); and drew on the findings to reflect on the implications for the future of school leadership and school as places of belonging (what kinds of leaders and leadership are needed?).

We approached the research in stages. In each of the sessions, we explored a different aspect of the challenges, feeding back their responses from the previous session at the start of each new one. Drawing on the guidelines of the British Education Research Association for the ethical conduct of research, we conducted 12 online workshops (four in each locality). The first three were held between May and July 2020, with a follow-up workshop in September 2020 to review our findings and discuss the transition back into full face-to-face schooling. The workshops were recorded. The headteachers also had the option of completing a diary exercise: 'A Day in My Life as a School Leader'.

In a context which provided these leaders with little time for reflection, this approach created an invaluable space for them to make sense of what they were seeing, experiencing and enacting. The climate of mutual support and trust which grew from this approach contributed to the sharing of experiences and learning, and enriched the research data. For these headteachers, participation in the collaboration was typically experienced in the following terms:

> Just to hear other voices of really experienced heads and how they have mitigated [the situation] has been incredibly useful, [even] instrumental in my mental health to survive this. I am feeling confident because I am listening to these voices and thinking about strategising, and I have legitimacy . . . These connections have been really helpful in making me feel competent.

As anxiety, fear and uncertainty grew in the local communities, the Covid-19 pandemic generated significant challenges for these 16 headteachers, as for their colleagues elsewhere. They found themselves holding the ring and struggling to manage the emotional overload; the requirements of government; and their own concerns about their school's reduced capacity to create a sense of belonging across the whole school community. Figure 8.1 offers an overview of how these school leaders experienced the immediate pressures and challenges of Covid-19.

In the early stages of lockdown, awareness of the unequal learning opportunities available to children, and the trauma facing communities, heightened levels of stress and emotional overload for them and their colleagues. As one headteacher reflected:

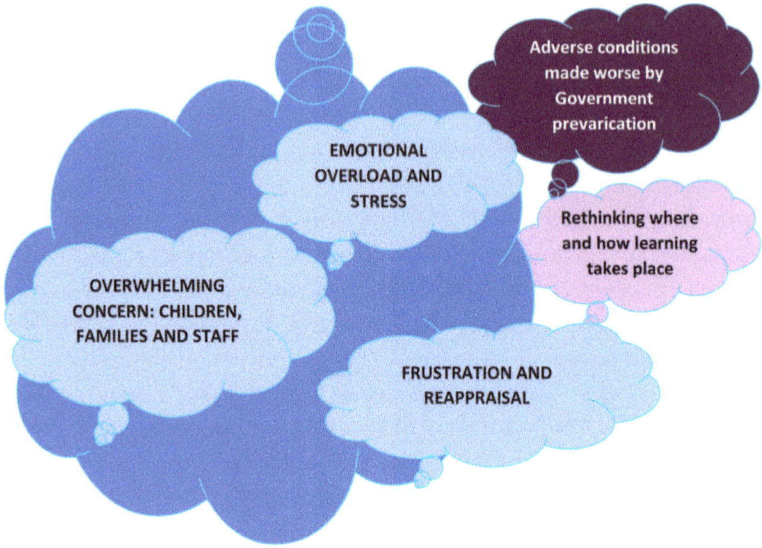

Figure 8.1 Leading in a new era: the first wave. Source: author.

> For the next year, we will be dealing with the children's feeling of death, because they had someone who died or because they feel they could die. We are going to be dealing with the effects of lockdown.

Governmental responses to the pandemic contributed to the challenges they faced, and the headteachers spoke of their frustration about information overload, lack of clarity and constantly changing information. They gave numerous examples of key Department for Education documents being emailed to them late at night; long and detailed guidance notes being amended, with the (headteacher) reader being left to trawl through to find the changes. They had concerns about an implied deficit model in government thinking about young people and were angry about the lack of appreciation of them, as highly trained professionals. They experienced a misalignment between their understanding of the crisis and its impact on children and communities, and governmental responses, directives, actions and inactions. The end result was a sense of facing the pandemic in a leaderless national climate. Professional networks provided a space to find solutions. Their local authorities offered practical support: how to deal with trauma, how to find your way through the government's maze of directives.

The experience of leading through the crisis also led this group of leaders to reappraise many taken-for-granted assumptions about relationships, policies and practices, and to become more flexible and adaptable in their approaches. In the section which follows, I have drawn on the 'Three Cs Framework' (see Figure 7.3) as a conceptual lens to shine a light on the motivation, decision-making and actions of this group of leaders over a period of some months.

The practice of compassion

In framing our first set of discussions with the headteachers, we introduced the notion of compassion, asking participants how compassionate they were to themselves. Did they accept the gaps in their knowledge? Their mistakes? Give themself time and space to breath?

Once the concept had been raised, compassion became a recurring theme: a language they chose to draw on. The pressures and anxieties of finding their way through lockdown had led them to think about their own leadership and to recognise that to be truly compassionate to other people, they first had to be compassionate to themselves. The willingness to acknowledge your own limitations ('I am not superwoman') was critical in circumstances which were unpredictable and unknowable:

> One of the things that has been really useful with my staff (during Covid-19) is saying that I don't have all the answers, I am not a superwoman, because this is all new. I am not God. It's about being compassionate. It's not about being the expert.

Acknowledging the pressures on them as leaders, and the importance of being compassionate to themselves, enabled them to find their own voice and recognise the concerns of others. What emerged was a recognition of the significance of their role in creating the school as a space of compassion: a place where members of the school community could support each other: 'Our philosophy is changing; it is a cultural change. We need to ask ourselves, how can we support each other as a community of headteachers and of teachers?'

However, this aspiration was constrained by the structural realities of a tightly regulated and highly competitive climate, defined by a narrowly based accountability system:

> Compassion does not necessarily work so well with those high levels of competition . . . We have had discussions about our feelings. There has been some very open sharing from our staff about racial trauma. But then you feel guilty that you are spending time on that and not on training academic skills . . . because of the competition.

The practice of connectivity

Positive forms of engagement generate the bedrock of relationships, as well as the networks needed to create a sense of place and belonging for young people and their families. Mutuality and trust between schools and their communities enable them to come together and weather many storms. The practice of leadership connectivity has two aspects: the first is about making connections with people; and the second is the willingness to see above and beyond the immediate. Both of these aspects of the practice of connectivity require an assertion of professional agency, and a commitment to enacting the agency of staff and students and bringing parents on board.

During the course of the research, we observed a growing assertion of the professional agency of this group of school leaders, reflected in the ways they spoke about the needs of their communities and their role in responding to those needs, as illustrated here.

> I had to have a conversation with myself and say, 'I know my children, I know my context, I know my school.' I think about my community . . . how can I adapt all of this to what they need? I've introduced a new programme on emotional resilience, nine hours in the first three weeks.

The need for social distancing, which had become paramount during the Covid-19 pandemic, reaffirmed the importance of building community. There was a shared commitment to finding new ways of connecting to families, and these school leaders were determined to know as much as they could about how their students felt, and what they and their families were experiencing.

These school leaders took practical steps to connect with students and their families, and to build community. They and their staff visited at a distance to drop off books. Schools created interactive video loops to stay connected, and messaged or phoned their students on a regular basis. Connectivity was expressed in many ways. It was about direct connections and connecting ideas: joining up the dots by challenging preconceptions and questioning taken-for-granted assumptions and practices. For some, the Black Lives Matter movement became the impetus for thinking about how to open up important but difficult conversations. One headteacher put this in the following terms:

> This is a moment in our lifetime when we can have open conversations about race and people can feel safe in expressing their opinions. It is an opportunity that we cannot miss . . . We have a duty to create that space of conversation and ensure that this space stays in place in our community.

He went on to argue that initiating such complex conversations also required some deep thinking about professional responsibilities:

> Think of how we have created prejudices. Think about the history of colonialism. We have talked about decolonialising the curriculum. How can we professionally move forward and occupy a space [on these matters]?

For other headteachers, the practice of connectivity was taking the opportunity to ask equally deep questions about the purpose of schooling. Lives and realities had been changed by the Covid-19 pandemic and developing children's reading skills had become more about enabling them to make sense of the world than meeting national achievement targets. This process of rethinking was deeply unsettling, but it also shaped new possibilities: 'We need to think of what life might be like when we return. There is a potential, an opportunity to create something better than we had before, to learn from the experience.'

The pandemic had put them, as leaders, face to face with the needs of communities at the cutting edge of society: those most exposed to its impact. Seeing above and beyond revealed new horizons.

> [There are] questions that have been around for some time but now have become more relevant. Schools play an important role in their communities . . . The question for me is: what I can do as a highly privileged person to change inequality and challenge oppression? How can I as a leader make things better for people in disadvantage? I am really interested in having this conversation.

By connecting their thoughts, practices and actions, these leaders found themselves in a stronger frame of mind to step into the emerging leadership space with added conviction.

The practice of communication

Connectivity is aligned to communication. As a leader, this is about reflecting on the messages that you want to convey, who you want to send those messages to, and how. These school leaders were united in a view that a central aspect of their role during the pandemic was to foster open and trust-based communications with staff and parents. Messages needed to be shared in open and inclusive ways with the school's wider community:

> We need to be able to have open conversations with parents and say, this is very complex, and you probably will be anxious when you come back. We cannot make teachers pretend that everything is alright. That is not reality. Everybody is looking for a solution to this problem, but the reality is that there is not a solution right now.

Building robust communications with parents throughout lockdown was dependent on establishing much more reciprocal relationships. As the 'lead' communicator, you had first to find your own voice before finding ways of bringing other voices into the frame – young people and their families, staff at all levels of the school.

> We really need to spend some time acknowledging what happened and try to build a sense of belonging . . . As a leader I think this is a really good opportunity to show that we care, so the parents know that we care about their children. I want my parents to be involved in school, develop those relationships. The parents make the school.

The many practical ways these headteachers had found to connect with the students and their families served to bring those families into the life of the school, and to create a sense of belonging and connectedness. Acknowledging the emotional overload for the whole school community, within and beyond the school walls, helped convey that the trauma is 'ours', as one headteacher reflected in the context of a community which had been brutally affected by the Covid-19 pandemic.

For these school leaders, communication became the enactment of connectivity: a recognition of the important role that schools have in creating community (outside the school) and of building community (within the school). The place called school needed to be characterised by mutual respect and actualised through a shared sense of belonging.

A sense of belonging generates confidence and a belief in the possibility of facing up to future challenges – within school and society. During a time of lockdown, the expectation of belonging needed to be nurtured so that when students walked into their classrooms again, or parents entered the school gates, they carried with them a sense of anticipation that they were arriving at a place where they belonged.

Leading out of lockdown: a new leadership space?

The picture which emerged from this study was not one of heroic leaders. This was not a story in which our superhero(ine) battles his or her way through the storm, with leadership as a solo endeavour. Nevertheless, we became deeply aware that the levels of physical and emotional commitment which these headteachers demonstrated daily – and without respite – take a personal toll that cannot be sustained in the long term. The findings raise many issues about the leaders we need for the future. How might they be supported as decision-makers? What do they need to be able to enact their agency as leaders? Reflecting on their experience of lockdown, these headteachers were all too keenly aware of the uncertainties which lay ahead. In what they perceived to be a political vacuum, the question they asked was: who should step into the leadership space and how?

> We are operating in this world of incredible frustrating unclarity. And the context keeps changing. That is very exhausting. Collectively creating community is challenging, and it is even more challenging when there is no clear information. In [this political vacuum] we need to create [our own] certainty and community.

As leaders during a global crisis, they had found new ways to listen and connect, as had their staff, and they did not want to lose these intangible and invaluable assets in the future. They recognised their own learning and that some of the strategies they had undertaken to reach out to families might not have taken place without the pandemic. For them, the future was about keeping the community connected and moving forward.

> There are things we've been wanting to change for a long time, but we haven't . . . This period has changed so many things, in a way it has been a positive learning experience. [It's time] to find other ways to make education fit for the twenty-first century.

Looking into the future and identifying what kinds of leadership are emerging, for these and other leaders, is a complex undertaking. In the spring of 2021, schools were due to reopen fully, and we met with the school leaders to take stock of their experiences. Were they coming up for air? Were they locked in a cloud of unknowing? They were all looking forward to the return of all their students and staff but were also exhausted. They recognised that while they had become skilful in riding the leadership wobble board, they had put all their energy into the Covid-19 sprint. Now they could see the marathon which still lay ahead and baulked at the implications for their time and energy. Figure 8.2 encapsulates how they felt.

They had learned much along the way but had found little time or space to capture their learning, or to plan how to incorporate what they and their colleagues had learned into what was to come. Their commitment to creating the conditions for school belonging was deeply rooted and strongly reinforced by their experience of the pandemic. Despite the feelings of stress and frustration, over time, a fresh articulation of what

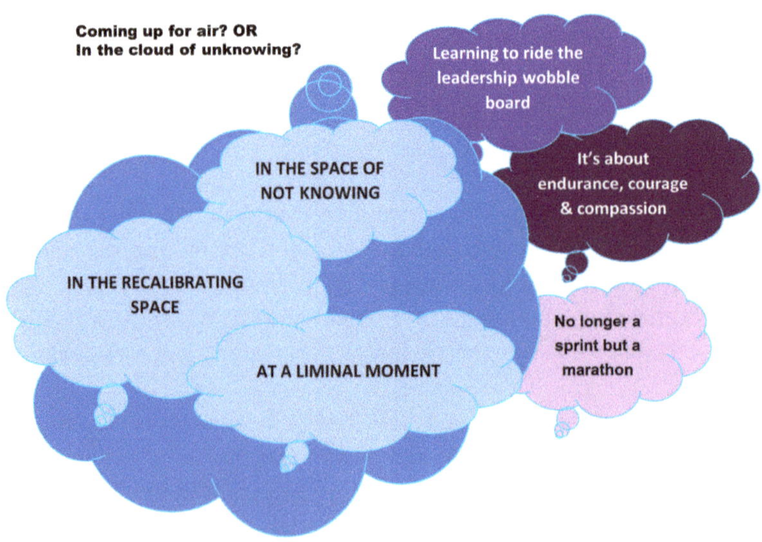

Figure 8.2 Leading in a new era: taking stock. Source: author.

schools are about, and how leaders can choose to lead, was emerging, which signals new possibilities about leadership.

For these school leaders, the experience of the pandemic had led to a strong sense of reaffirmation: that first and foremost, children and young people needed to be seen for who they are, rather than as the grades they are projected to achieve. This experience had encouraged them to articulate the notion of leadership as a moral endeavour – a dynamic ministry, as others have argued (Smylie, Murphy and Seashore 2020) – and to step into a view of leadership as a highly relational and place-based activity, driven by deep wells of compassion. The language of belonging, compassion and connectivity had come centre stage. One headteacher concluded that to build the conditions for school belonging, she had first to build a place 'where the students have a voice and . . . feel that they are part of the school, that they are not afraid to give their opinion even if it is something different . . . not afraid of not being like the others'.

9
Reframing 'what is' to 'what can be'

> I was thinking about all the people who are actually involved in a school – the pupils, the teachers, the teaching assistants, all of those people. If they all thought about their school in a different way – a place where I go, a place where I feel I belong, where I feel I can contribute, where I feel like what I say is heard, what a dynamic wonderful place that would be.
> (Rhoda Furniss, quoted in Riley 2017: 142)

Mariana stands at the threshold of school life, eagerly awaiting what is to come (Figure 9.1). Her sense of joyful anticipation reaches to the very tips of her fingers. 'I belong here', she writes, vividly depicting how she sees her school as a place of welcome and belonging. Yet the dawn of a new school day brings anxiety and dread for too many children and young people.

This chapter steps back from the immediacy of the data to look at the wider landscape and the conditions needed to create school belonging and offers a reframing of 'what is' to 'what can be'. While this is not a magic potion derived from some long-hidden spell, it is based on solid evidence. This analysis draws on findings from a cross-sector collaborative inquiry on the changes in policy and practice needed to create school belonging which brought together eight partner organisations in the United Kingdom from health, schools, teacher education, social policy, local authorities and the voluntary sector: the Education Policy Institute; the Difference; the Institute of Health Sciences Education; Community-Based Medical Education, Barts; Mulberry School for Girls, Tower Hamlets; the National Education Union; Teach First; Telford and Wrekin Council; the Refugee Support Network; and a team from the UCL Institute of Education (Riley, Mendoza and Gonzales, 2020).

Figure 9.1 I belong here (Riley, Coates and Allen, 2020).

We live in strange and uncertain times. Our lives have been disrupted in ways we could scarcely have envisaged, and the future lies ahead, unknown and unknowable. The pandemic juggernaut has put governments to the test, and some have fared better than others. Under the weight of many uncertainties, much of what had been taken for granted about how schools function has been turned on its head. Conventional practices and assumptions have been questioned about how the school day is organised, where and how teaching and learning takes place, or who is involved in the process. The pack of cards which make up the pattern of school life has been tossed high into the air and has yet to fall to the ground. When it does, there are choices to be made. The cards can be returned to their previous order, or they can be rearranged and reordered.

This chapter shines a spotlight on the processes of rethinking, reconnecting and recalibrating needed at different levels of the education system to make a difference. The focus is on the possibilities which can emerge from a reconfiguring of 'what is' to 'what can be': the actions needed to create that move away from the status quo (the seemingly inexorable rise in exclusions and in a sense of feeling marginalised), to a different set of realities in which Mariana's experiences become the norm.

The evidence about school belonging presented in this book indicates that children and young people who feel they belong in school tend to be happier and more confident and also perform better academically.

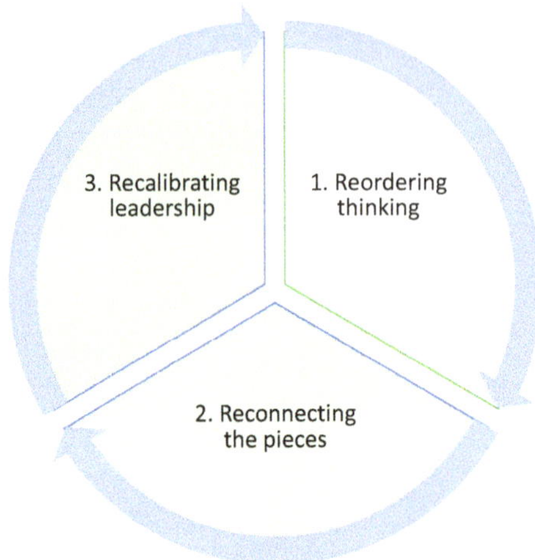

Figure 9.2 The 'Reordering, Reconnecting, Recalibrating Jigsaw'. Source: author.

For many young people, belonging is their everyday (very positive) reality. The challenge becomes how to expand that experience to include a much wider group of young people. The changes needed to make this happen are far from insurmountable; the potential gains are incalculable. I have organised this final discussion around three interconnected elements of the 'Reordering, Reconnecting, Recalibrating Jigsaw' (Figure 9.2).

Reordering thinking

How to change the mindset by moving away from school systems which are dominated by dogmas of order, control and excessive competition that constrain and limit thinking and practice.

The assumption that schools are about order, and leadership is about control, has emerged over a number of years. In an earlier study (Riley 1998), I looked at events at William Tyndale primary school, a *cause célèbre* of its day in the 1970s. William Tyndale came to be seen, by some, as a school where left-wing teachers had tried to give working-class children real choices (Ellis et al. 1976), and by others as a school out of control (Auld 1976). This latter view was endorsed by the prime minister of the day, James Callaghan, whom I interviewed for my book (Riley 1998).

In 1976 Callaghan delivered a speech at Ruskin College, Oxford University, in which he expressed his disquiet about the state of education.

His Ruskin speech came to be seen as a watermark in education thinking. Its content was influenced by his personal take on a number of events, including Tyndale and the student protests of the late 1960s, which he considered to be a waste of the taxes of ordinary working-class people. A narrative emerged which was one of dysfunctionality, an educational system out of control.

Over the years which followed, the policy response to this narrative, from a succession of governments, included the introduction of new forms of accountability, high-stakes testing and tough sanctions-based behaviour policies which have contributed to the contemporary climate of rising rates of school exclusions, and to the growth in the number of young people who feel that they do not belong in school (Riley 1998).

Undoubtedly there are occasions in which order and control are needed. There are non-negotiable issues about physical safety – the need to evacuate a building or ensure that children and adults keep a safe distance during a pandemic, for example. However, when order takes over as the prevailing imperative and the essence of school life becomes about control, different voices are ignored. Identities are subsumed into a collective pot. Practices are condoned that ignore young people's sense of self and identity, and the richness of the experiences of the diverse lives which make up any school community are lost. As a consequence, frustrations mount and dissonance can emerge among those whose voices are ignored. When order becomes a weapon of control, it impedes the essential harmony of school life.

This challenge to 'order and control' is not a vote for 'disorder', an education free-for-all. Anarchy creates its own inequities, dysfunctionalities and victims. However, the boundaries generated by a culture of order and control not only constrain thinking but can also lead to a culture of inaction that is manifested in many ways. It includes the failure to recognise, challenge or intervene in the actions of staff or pupils, which can contribute to the 'othering' or ostracisation of children and young people, or to the worrying increase in sexual abuse in UK schools, as discussed in Chapter 2.

One of the most disturbing findings from a national report on this rise in sex abuse in school has been the degree to which some schools have seemingly been unaware of the toxic environment in their school, or the level of the abuse (Ofsted 2021). The young people in those schools did not feel that they had a voice or chose not to speak out because they thought that their voice would not be listened to. This is an indication of major system failure.

It is important to recognise, however, that over time, different parts of *any* system can drift off course and will need to be reset. This is as true of a navigation system as a school system. Undoubtedly, some parts of our school system have lost their bearings. Recognising that the school system is adrift and needs fresh coordinates is a major challenge. A first step forward is to acknowledge the scale of the problem of exclusion and alienation, and a second is to recognise the importance of developing young people's sense of agency and personal responsibility. In these fragile times, we need to take advantage of this precious moment to introduce a new reference point which will help us navigate our way through uncertain times: that of belonging.

Reconnecting the pieces

How to identify the contours on the horizon which represent the most significant points of positive intervention and action, within schools and across school systems.

Reordering our thoughts and adding a new reference point will enable us to scan the horizon with fresh energy, and see the contours and connections in thinking and practice needed to bring about change. In 2009, practitioners from education, health and social policy in the United States came together in an initiative known as the Wingspread Declaration on School Connections (American School Health Association 2009) to share their knowledge and understanding about the policies and practices most likely to help create a sense of connectiveness and belonging in school for young people. Strategies identified as being most likely to create that sense of belonging and connectivity included high standards, expectations and support for all students; fair and consistent disciplinary policies; trusting relationships; skilled teachers who focused on meeting the needs of learners; strategies which fostered high parent/family expectations; and approaches which ensure that every student feels close to at least one supportive adult at school (American School Health Association 2009). These actions are consistent with many of the findings about belonging reported in this book.

Looking more broadly, there are a number of potential points of intervention and action at the different levels of education systems – national, system and school level – which can help create that sense of connectivity and belonging. Figure 9.3 summarises some of the points of intervention and the key features of a strategic approach which is intentional, consistent and connected.

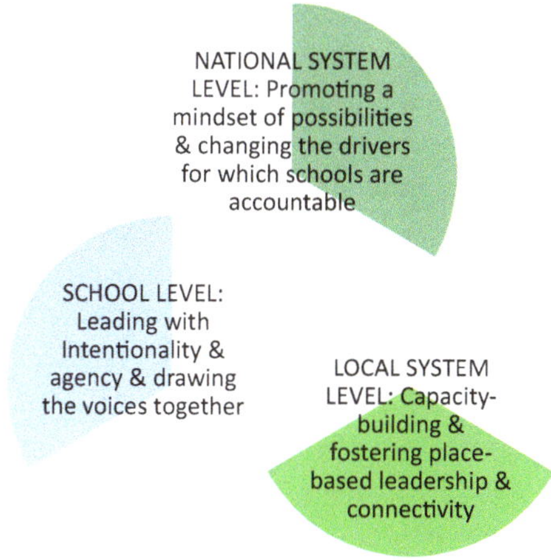

Figure 9.3 Place and belonging: connecting the system.
Source: author.

National system level

Governments set the tone about what is expected and what is possible through the messages they send about who and what is important. By dint of financial directives, as well as rewards and sanctions, they shape what happens in schools. The policy dialogue frames the language of belonging and inclusion, while specific policies have an impact on the levels of exclusion of young people from school. However, what will have the deepest impact on practice is a fundamental shift in the mindset: from a mindset of control to one of possibilities.

The expression of such a shift would be reflected in a change in the broad policy drivers which characterise the accountability relationship. In the English system, this would be experienced as a shift from the *transactional* (here are the results your students need to get) to the *aspirational* (here is how your students can fulfil themselves and contribute to society). This change in the mindset would include encouragement for schools to move away from traditional behaviour management approaches (with their over-emphasis on rewards and sanctions), towards more humanist, relational and universal approaches which are inclusive for all. External systems of scrutiny would come to focus on measures of inclusivity and belonging, for young people and staff. System planning would foster intentional, purposeful and positive interventions – rather than one-off reactions – that are clearly understood across the school system.

Local system level

The middle level tier in any education system is key. When working well and effectively, it provides the mediating bridge between national policy-makers and school communities and becomes a source of support for school leaders. Local systems – be they local authorities, municipalities or school boards or chains – come into their own when interventions are agreed and targeted, and there is a consistent effort to develop the capacity of staff and local agencies and bring diverse voices together. When local systems support the development of place-based, compassionate and intentional leadership – which recognises the distinctiveness of localities and encourages the involvement of young people and communities – the effect is to harness the social capital of local communities, which often lies untapped.

Telford and Wrekin, in Shropshire, England, is a cooperative council and found itself facing endemic and recurring issues about inclusion, exclusion and behaviour. Fixed-term exclusions were growing, more children were entering care and there was a rise in the demand for support for children with mental health issues. In response to this, Heather Loveridge, past director of education and skills at Telford and Wrekin Council, was asked to lead a review on behaviour. She then had what she described to me as her 'light bulb moment'. Influenced by work on place and belonging (Riley 2017, 2019a, 2019b), she concluded that the authority was going about things in 'the same tired old way' and needed to look at things afresh, through the 'Prism of place and belonging' (see Chapter 6). That light bulb moment led to the development of Telford and Wrekin's Belonging Strategy and to the creation of its ambition: 'Every child – will have a sense of belonging' (Telford and Wrekin Council 2019).

The Telford strategy incorporates the priorities for increasing a sense of belonging, as well as the success measures which include reduced exclusions and referrals to targeted services; reduced dropout rates at Year 12; and increased mental health and emotional resilience. Mental health issues, domestic abuse and alcohol misuse can all contribute to the way a child might behave, Heather argues. Based on a partnership with schools, Telford's Belonging Strategy also details the approaches that schools can take to understand more about young people's needs (such as autism awareness training), as well as the system-wide strategies (such as connecting services dealing with mental health) which could make a significant difference. Behind the strategy is the recognition that a connected and systematic approach is needed if different partners are to be brought together, and the totality of young people's lives acknowledged. This process of local connectivity is made more difficult by the ways in which national policies place schools in competition with each other.

In 2019, Ofsted (the Office for Standards in Education, Children's Services and Skills is a non-ministerial department of the UK government) rated Telford and Wrekin Council's education and children's services as 'outstanding'. Ofsted inspectors commended the council's Belonging Strategy for its holistic response to the issues of inclusion and belonging. In 2020, headteachers from Telford and Wrekin taking part in 'Leadership in a New Era' – reported in the previous chapter – described how Telford's Belonging Strategy had helped create a bedrock of shared understanding which had supported them, as school leaders, during the Covid-19 crisis. The headteachers from Hackney and Islington also valued the support and connectivity of their local authorities. The example of Telford and Wrekin Council illustrates the ways in which a localised, system-wide approach can help create a shared set of aspirations and actions.

School level

The school is a key site for fostering belonging, and many examples of how this operates in practice have been given throughout the book. A sense of belonging is as important for staff as for young people. Schools where behaviour is poor, and where responses to behaviour are punitive, are as debilitating for staff as students. Creating school belonging requires intention, purpose and a commitment to connectedness. Relationships are at the heart of what makes a difference.

The evidence at the school level is that young people flourish in school climates which are inclusive and rooted in the joy of learning, and the thrill of creativity. In schools of belonging, trusting relationships prevail: between teachers and students, teachers and school leaders, school staff and families. Leadership is place-based, compassionate and intentional, and leaders work to bring together the many voices within a school community.

Recalibrating leadership

How to support the development of relational and place-based forms of leadership, driven by deep wells of compassion, which can help cultivate positive and inclusive school climates of school belonging.

To help tackle system drift and create the conditions for school belonging, the third element in the jigsaw is to recalibrate leadership. Figure 9.4 maps the three stages of this challenging recalibration process for school leaders. The school leaders who were part of the research reported in the previous chapter had looked at the leadership at a national level and found it woefully lacking. In response to the Covid-19 pandemic, they were working to recalibrate their own leadership, a difficult process. What had they learned?

In the first stages of the pandemic, they had found themselves in the place of 'not knowing': a place where all the cards were up in the air. Those leaders who saw their role as being able to plan had found this a difficult and uncomfortable space to occupy. Most went on to find themselves in a second liminal stage, an in-between moment when they began to ask themselves the big questions about what matters in schools. In this liminal stage, it may feel possible to cross the threshold into a new leadership reality, but there is continuing anxiety about the unknown. Finally, there is a recalibrating space in which old certainties have been left behind and new possibilities emerge. This is where a number of members of this group of leaders appeared to be heading.

Re-calibrating leadership is about working through the space of not knowing >< entering the liminal moment >< and then arriving in the recalibrating space.

Leadership has always been an uncertain business, but today even more so. The reality of the future is unknown and unknowable. Attempts to

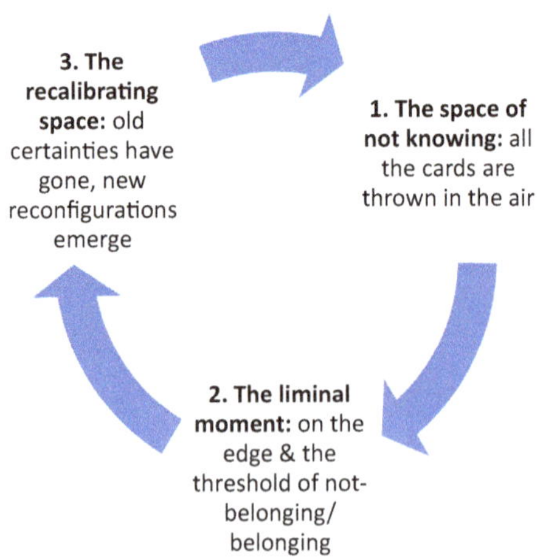

Figure 9.4 The emerging spaces. Source: author.

find certainty when there is none add to the stress. It is hard as a leader to feel safe and secure when you *do not know*, and want others to feel safe. The leadership challenge becomes how to lead others into, and through, the unknown. Some of the complexities of this complex process of thinking through the emerging spaces are highlighted below.

The space of not knowing can be uncomfortable, disconcerting and frightening. From being a leader who knows what needs to happen – each school year, term, week – and who knows his or her role in shaping that, the certainty about what to do, or the sense that as the leader you should know the answers, has dissipated. Accepting as a leader that you don't know becomes part of the job, and those who struggle to come to terms with this may find themselves adrift.

The liminal moment can also be as disconcerting a place to occupy as a leader as the 'space of not knowing'. When leaders feel that they are in a liminal or transitional place, they may feel they do not belong, yet their role as a leader is to bring other people into belonging. In the liminal space, leaders are at the threshold of not knowing where they are or where they are going, and crossing the threshold to a new space. All the cards have been thrown up in the air. They may fall differently. They can be played differently. As the seeds of future possibilities lie in the liminal space, it can become a space of positive anticipation.

In *the recalibrating space*, old certainties have gone and new reconfigurations are emerging, such as new forms of relational leadership. There are the possibilities of strengthening partnerships with families and communities; and the opportunities to bring disparate voices on board and to create compassionate communities in which young people and staff have a sense of connectivity and belonging.

The compassionate way

The school leaders interviewed for the research presented in the previous chapter are learning to ride the new leadership wobble board, although finding it a daunting task. What was once seen as an annual leadership sprint is now being recognised as more of a marathon. Compassion has kept them going. Compassion is the superglue that can bring school leaders, staff, families and communities together. It is the ingredient which has the potential to redress some of the imbalances and inequities revealed by the pandemic. Compassion brings joy to the lives of young people, creating bonds and friendships in a shared community of learners, as is expressed in Figure 9.5. Compassionate leaders recognise uncertainty and accept that while they as leaders may not know *what* is going to happen in the future, they do know *why* they want to work with families and communities and *how* to make schools places of belonging.

The 'Three Cs Framework' of compassion, connectivity and communication offers a way forward. It is a touchstone for thinking about the kinds of leadership needed to create school belonging. The magnitude of compassion which underpins this framework is a belief in possibilities and the recognition of the importance of compassionate, relational, place-based leadership.

This chapter began with an inspirational quotation which captures the power of belief and the realisation of possibilities. If we all thought about schools in a different way, as Rhoda Furniss argued, what amazing places they could be. Seeing things differently, and with fresh clarity, is the first step along the way to completing the 'Reordering, Reconnecting, Recalibrating Jigsaw'.

Figure 9.5 Coming together. Source: author.

Reflection

This book has touched upon the many ways in which young people can become ostracised, excluded or alienated by their school experiences. It has also given a flavour of what school belonging looks like and how school leaders can choose to enact their leadership in compassionate ways that will help grow school belonging. Figure X.1 represents a key set of relationships and connections. Leadership *values* shape *action*, and leadership *actions* shape *belonging*. Compassionate leadership is expressed through the degree to which the conditions for school belonging are put into place by leaders.

Educational leaders – be they policymakers or practitioners at senior levels within a school, or classroom leaders – are in the privileged position of being able to enact their leadership. They can choose to do this in a highly relational and compassionate way that seeks to make connections and bring a wide range of voices on board. Or they can see their role as being fulfilled by the number of instructions they give, or directions they follow. However, hiding behind directives will do little to improve the life chances of young people.

Schools' practices have a significant impact on young people's lives, generating a climate of inclusion, exclusion or rejection. Meaningful and equitable partnerships between schools and their communities can change beliefs and practices. A sense of belonging is generated and manifested in the ways in which staff and students listen and respond to each other and talk about each other. Schools which are places of belonging are great places to be, for young people and staff, and places of welcome for families and communities.

While the extremes of the Covid-19 crisis are likely to diminish over time, we will be living with its emotional, social, economic and educational consequences for many years to come. Some school systems may choose to return to 'business as usual': the reimposition of highly regulated and controlled structures, the introduction of programmes couched in the deficit language of bringing 'kids' back on track, which seems to imply that the young people have failed in some way. However, attempts to reinstate

Figure X.1 Values, actions and a sense of belonging. Source: author.

the status quo of previous years are likely to lead to significant increases in levels of exclusion, alienation and failure. Choosing to search for alternatives becomes, as Yuval Noah Harari has argued, a way of building 'global solidarity' and new options for future generations (Harari 2020).

The pandemic has affected us all, pushing us to rethink the power dynamics and relationships both within schools, and between schools and communities. Old certainties have gone. Young people's lives and expectations have been shaken in ways that we are yet to fully comprehend. The intensity of the 2020–22 crisis; ongoing uncertainties about the social and economic landscape; growing mental health issues; the powerful messages of the Black Lives Matter movement – all these serve as a wake-up call. Tackling exclusion and alienation can no longer remain on the back burner.

The final vignette in the book takes us back to Redvil Primary School, a school visited in Chapter 5. It describes one of those moments when we come to experience the essence of what school belonging feels like – for young people, their teachers, their families and for visiting academics!

Vignette 7: The 'bestseatsinthehouse' Assembly: Redvil Primary School, Northeast England

It is February 2020 and a wintry Friday afternoon in Leeds. The rain is pouring down. Pushing buggies and clutching umbrellas, parents and grandparents pick their way gingerly through the puddles of Redvil's steep playground to reach the school's entrance. The school is hosting its weekly 'bestseatsinthehouse' assembly, which celebrates the achievements of their children, sharing this with their families. I have been invited too.

The children compete to show how great they are – at spelling and tables, geography and science, any aspect of their school life. Their achievements are met with cheers and rounds of applause.

One of the stars of the week is Maya. Her teacher is sitting near me and stands up with great pride to introduce Maya as she is called to the front. Smiling at her, she says: 'Maya, where do I start? She's a lovely girl, caring and hard-working. She has a positive attitude to everything that she does. She is hungry to learn. She's a credit to her parents and herself.' An assortment of Maya's relatives are in the audience in that packed school hall, the same hall which was empty when the headteacher held his first parents' evening. They cannot stop beaming and clapping.

Winners from the 'bestseatsinthehouse' assembly spill out into the hallway, eager to spend their awards on the new vending machine. However, it is a vending machine with a difference, not fizzy drinks or crisps but books: the classics, *The Three Musketeers*, mysteries of the past, *The Totally Dead Dinosaurs* and the chocolate fix, *Charlie and the Chocolate Factory*.

The sound is deafening. If you could bottle the energy, you could light up the whole estate.

Wisdom and compassion help build connections and communities. A moment in time exists in which it is possible to move forward with creating the conditions which will enable young people and adults to feel welcome and accepted in school. Aspirations can become realities. The possibility of constructing a different reality exists. These possibilities can be found today in those schools which are working to develop reciprocal relationships with families and create school communities in which young people can feel safe in their own skin and comfortable in their identity.

Evidence of the success of these approaches presented in this book offers encouragement to other school leaders and policymakers to engage in intentional, purposeful and compassionate leadership. The narrative which will support such approaches is based on a belief in possibilities. Conditions are ripe for compassionate leadership to spring up at all levels across the school system, at a policy level, within schools and within classrooms. Nevertheless, some leaders may need to reset their moral compass and refresh their navigational skills to be able to do this.

Whether children and young people feel connected to their school and experience a sense of belonging and agency will influence how they think about themselves today, and how they see their future on our planet as global citizens. Schools can and should be places of joy, wonder and inquiry. We have the knowledge and skills to create the conditions for this to happen. All that is needed is the will.

Appendix 1: Research on place and belonging

This appendix offers a short synthesis of 10 examples of the author's own research on place and belonging, carried out in partnership with a number of co-researchers, referred to in the book. The research is summarised in Table A1.

Table A.1 Research on place and belonging

Title	Date	Scope
Study 1: 'Working with Disaffected Students' (Riley and Rustique-Forrester, 2002)	2001–2	The two-year study focused on inclusion, exploring the causes and dynamics of pupil disaffection and disengagement from school, and identifying the factors which make a positive difference to how pupils on the margins experience school life. The study was conducted in partnership with Lancashire local authority. Forty-five young people – all of whom had been excluded from school – were involved, as well as 140 teachers, school leaders and parents. Data was collected through interviews, focus groups and drawing exercises with young people.
Study 2: 'Leadership on the Front Line' (Riley and Emery 2007; Riley 2007, 2008)	2002–6	The four-year study focused on place: what it meant to be a school leader and what was going on for young people, both within school and in the local community. It involved 70 headteachers/principals from primary, secondary and special schools, located in highly disadvantaged areas in Belfast, Birmingham, Cardiff, London, Londonderry, Liverpool, Manchester, Salford, Dublin and Paris. Headteacher data was collected through interviews and leadership diary logs, and through discussions and activities at a series of collaborative conferences. Nearly 200 young people participated in the drawing exercises about schools and communities.

Table A.1 (*Continued*)

Study 3: 'Leadership of Place' (Riley 2013a)	2010–12	The study explored how school leaders in three countries and localities – the United States (Brooklyn, New York); the UK (London's East End) and South Africa (the Eastern Cape) – thought about and enacted their leadership, both within the school and the wider community. It explored the school and non-school realities for more than 100 young people from 15 primary and secondary schools, the majority of whom were growing up in impoverished communities. Data was collected through interviews, focus groups and drawing exercises.
Study 4: 'Effective Principals Serving in High Poverty Schools in Chile' (Riley, Montecinos and Ahumada 2016)	2014–15	This research focused on the leadership challenges facing principals in Chile and how they enacted their leadership. Case studies were undertaken of three principals leading public elementary schools in Chile.The schools were serving socially and economically disadvantaged communities and were deemed to be 'successful' on a range of criteria. Data was collected through interviews, documentary analysis, and a drawing exercise which involved some 80 children.
Study 5: 'School: A Place Where I Belong?' (Riley 2017)	2014–16	The question at the heart of this study was: 'Is this school a place where everyone feels they belong?' Based on a process of collaborative research inquiry, the research explored how a sense of place and belonging is experienced and generated, and the impact of researching about place and belonging for those involved and their schools. The study involved 35 primary and secondary school student-researchers and 36 teacher-researchers (newly qualified teachers) from 13 London schools, all located in challenging urban contexts. The student- and teacher-researchers undertook a range of data gathering activities, including surveys, drawings and interviews. The UCL Institute of Education team trained and supported the school-based researchers, undertook headteacher interviews and hosted seminars and workshops.

Table A.1 (*Continued*)

Title	Date	Scope
Study 6: 'Place and Space' (Riley, Coates and Martinez 2018)	2017	This exploratory study was organised around a leadership research hub of headteachers/school principals and aspiring leaders. It traced how school leaders developed their role as place-makers and place leaders, seeking to identify the strategies likely to encourage other leaders – at different levels within the school – to see themselves in these roles and the tools which would help them do this.
Study 7: 'Place and Belonging in School: Why It Matters Today': case studies (Riley, Coates and Allen 2020)	2019–20	Research commissioned by the National Education Union, involving five schools, their headteachers, 49 teachers and teaching assistants and 79 children and young people. The study aimed to explore the links between a sense of belonging, behaviour and learning outcomes. Findings have much to offer about the practice of school belonging, the characteristics of schools where belonging works, and the actions which pupils, staff and school leaders can take to make a difference.
Study 8: 'Place and Belonging in School: Why It Matters Today': literature review (Allen, Riley and Coates 2020)	2019–20	This literature review aimed to expand understanding of the connections between belonging, behaviour and inclusion in school. It looked, in particular, at the evidence about the effectiveness of sanction-driven approaches to behaviour management and the impact of relational-based, whole school strategies and interventions.

Table A.1 (*Continued*)

Study 9: 'Leadership in a New Era' (Riley and Mendoza 2020)	2020	'Leading in a New Era' was constructed in partnership with three local authorities: Telford and Wrekin Council (which is northwest of Birmingham), the East London borough of Hackney and the North London borough of Islington (Riley and Mendoza 2020). While each of the local authority areas has its own distinctive demographic and economic characteristics, all three were committed to inclusive practices and creative pedagogic approaches. The research involved 16 headteachers (11 female and 5 male) who came from primary, secondary and special needs schools. Some were headteachers of long standing – executive heads or on their second headship – others were 'fledgling heads' in their first year of headship. The core research activities took place between April and July 2020, a four-month period of lockdown during the Covid-19 crisis. While schools were open for the children of key workers and for young people with particular needs, the majority of students attended online or through distance learning. Follow-up discussions with the headteachers continued in September and December 2020, when schools were back to face-to-face teaching, and in January 2021. The picture which emerged from this study was not one of heroic leaders but of leadership motivated by compassion, caring and place-making, designed to build community and create a sense of belonging.
Study 10: 'Cross-Sector and Interdisciplinary Perspectives on School Belonging and Exclusion' (Riley, Mendoza and Gonzales 2020)	2019–21	A cross-sector collaborative inquiry coordinated by the UCL Institute of Education, involving eight partner institutions. The aims were to: (i) identify the interventions, practices and system-wide changes in policy and practice needed to create school belonging; (ii) draw together the silos of knowledge about the impact of exclusion, disaffection and alienation on children and young people around one broader shared and positive narrative – that of belonging; and (iii) identify the system-wide issues and implications for policy and practice.

Appendix 2: Research methodology and further tools

This appendix provides further information about the research study 'Place and Belonging in School: Why It Matters Today' (Riley, Coates and Allen 2020), which is discussed in Chapter 6, as well as details of one of the research tools used, a card-sort exercise on belonging. The research included interviews, group discussions with staff and a drawing exercise.

The semi-structured interviews with the headteachers were designed to elicit information about the policies and practices which they thought helped increase children and young people's sense of belonging in school and were recorded. We discussed the school and community context; understandings of belonging; the nature of the school's engagement with the wider community; the strategies used to build a school community; and evidence about the degree to which a community of belonging had been created.

Group discussions with staff revolved around two themes: behaviour polices (how were they constructed and understood?); and school belonging (did students and staff feel a sense of belonging? How was belonging articulated and enacted?). As a trigger for this discussion about belonging, we used a card-sort exercise with statements about belonging derived from research. We used a drawing exercise as a prompt for the discussion with young people, asking: 'What does it look like (in my school) when I feel that I belong?' 'What does it look like (in my school) when I feel that I don't belong?'

Research tool: card-sort exercise on school belonging

This card-sort exercise is an example of the kinds of qualitative research tools which can be used to explore issues about place and belonging. I first began using a card-sort methodology in joint work with Karen Seashore

Louis on school–community collaboration. Based on a rigorous literature review, we used it as a tool to understand the perspectives of young people, school leaders and community members, adjusting the wording for each group. The card-sort exercise included here was intended as a prompt for understanding teachers' perspectives on school belonging and was developed in partnership with Dr Max Coates. The literature on belonging which underpins it is incorporated into the book.

As a methodology, a card-sort exercise is a rich way to understand the beliefs and actions of participants. As a group exercise it is very inclusive – every participant has space. As a reflective exercise, with no right or wrong answers, participants seem comfortable in raising issues that are deeply important to them and which they may not have articulated before, as emerged in the discussion with teachers reported in Chapter 5. As an analytical exercise it helps connect the research to a range of theoretical and conceptual understandings in the work of other authors.

Information for participants

1. **Core script**: We are here today because we are particularly interested in your thinking about two important matters:

    - What you think about the importance of schools as places of belonging.
    - What we can learn from you about those activities, approaches and interventions which contribute to positive outcomes for young people, their families and school communities.

    Our research today is sponsored by the NEU. It follows on from previous work on place, belonging, inclusion and exclusion. We are working with a number of other schools in England, and hopefully elsewhere, and plan to share what we learn from you with a wide audience. We won't name you individually but will name your school.

2. **The exercise:** On your sheet you have nine statements about belonging. They all come from research. Your first task is to cut out your statements. You will also see that you have a blank statement so that you can add anything else of importance.

When you have had a chance to look at the statements, we would like you to think about what is most important to you. This is not a test – there are no right or wrong answers! We would like you to make a diamond. The most important statement goes at the top and the least important at the bottom. Those on the same line are of equal importance.

- Line one has one statement – the most important.
- Line two has two statements / Line 3 – three / Line 4 – two / Line 5 – one.

Each statement begins as follows: 'A sense of belonging is important in this school because . . .' Let us talk about you have done. Why did you make your choices? Is there a 10th statement you would like to add?

3. **Reflections:** Building on what you have said, let me ask you one final question. It has two parts: (i) How do you apply your thinking about belonging to what you do in this school? (ii) What more could you do?

Information for the research team

1. **What is the core purpose of the exercise?** This is designed as a reflective exercise aimed at promoting an open discussion which reflects the culture of the school. We are exploring beliefs, assumptions and practices and intent. How do participants:

    - See the issues?
    - Think about them?
    - Act in response to this?

2. **How are we structuring the exercise?** Drawing on some of the key principles of the Diamond 9 approach, which is used to promote discussion in an open and equitable manner. Nine statements have been developed which are drawn from the literature on the impact of a sense of belonging. Participants can add a 10th.

3. **What are we trying to find out by the end of the session?**

- How are issues about belonging thought about, articulated, experienced and acted on?
- Is there a common language and a shared set of practices?
- How do staff think about behaviour issues? For example, are there any indications of a move away from traditional behaviour management approaches (emphasis on rewards and sanctions) towards more humanist, relational and universal approaches?
- Is there an underpinning philosophy (e.g. every child – a sense of belonging: a place to succeed?)
- What have we learned about the language of belonging?

The nine statements

A sense of belonging is important in this school because . . .

1. When you feel you belong you can be more creative, innovative and confident.
2. Belonging is about being respected and feeling accepted.
3. It helps you feel part of the community – part of society.
4. When children feel safe and that they belong, their attendance improves and so does their academic performance.
5. Belonging is about feeling that you are valued and are part of a place.
6. It contributes significantly to developing good mental health and a feeling of wellbeing.
7. When staff feel that they belong, it helps retention – they'll stay in the school.
8. When you feel you belong, you can be yourself; you can develop your own sense of personal identity.
9. When you can grow and develop your sense of belonging in school, you learn how to be yourself and fit in elsewhere.

These nine statements are all linked to research. For example, statement 2 is derived from Goodenow and Grady (1993) on the extent to which students feel personally accepted, respected, included and supported by others in the school social environment.

Examples of other useful research tools and methodological frameworks used to explore issues around place and belonging include:

- 'Taking the leadership pulse' (Riley 2007)
- 'Preparing student-researchers' (Riley 2017: Appendix II)
- 'A leader's guide to researching for place and belonging' (Riley 2017: Figure 9.3:)
- 'Belonging as a dynamic concept' (Riley, Coates and Perez Martinez 2018: Box 3)
- 'An educational design research model for creating a sense of place and belonging – the art of possibilities' (Riley, Coates and Perez Martinez 2018: Box 4).

Appendix 3: Videos and materials linked to place and belonging

Many of the ideas discussed in the book are supported by linked materials and videos in the Art of Possibilities Series. These are available at The Art of Possibilities (www.theartofpossibilities.org.uk).

Series I: The Art of Possibilities (Dida Media)

These five videos are linked to the research project 'School: A Place Where I Belong?' and illustrate key themes in Kathryn Riley's 2017 book, *Place Belonging and School Leadership*.

- Place, Belonging and Schools in our Global World
- A Place to Be: Student-Researchers Show the Way
- Rethinking Classrooms: Teacher-Researchers Learn from their Students
- Using Poetry Performance to Create Place and Belonging
- Making Belonging Work in a Volatile World

Series II: The Art of Possibilities: Place and Belonging in Schools (SpectreCom Films)

The videos in this series illustrate something of the practice of school belonging and introduce key concepts and practices which can support school belonging.

- Belonging (St Anthony's Catholic Primary School)
- Agency

- Place and Space
- Unlocking Possibilities

Series III: The Art of Possibilities (edited and produced by The Art of Possibilities)

The first of these two videos is linked to a Deptford-based community project, 'Deptford: A World of Possibilities', and the second to work in Morocco linked to a keynote presentation at ICSEI 2020 in Marrakesh.

- Reaching Deptford
- The Power of Belonging (Morocco)

References

Abdollahi, A., Panahipour, S., Tafti, M.A., and Allen, K.A. (2020) 'Academic hardiness as a mediator for the relationship between school belonging and academic stress'. *Psychology in the Schools*. https://doi.org/10.1002/pits.22339.

Ainscow, M., Muijs, D., and West, M. (2006) 'Collaboration as a strategy for improving schools in challenging circumstances'. *Improving Schools* 9 (3), 192–202.

Albrow, M. (2015) *The Global Age: State and society beyond modernity*. Cambridge: Polity, 1996.

Alexander, T. (2013) *Citizenship Schools: Learning democracy, raising attainment, building community*. Manchester: Cooperative College.

Allen, K.A. (2020) *Psychology of Belonging*. London: Routledge.

Allen, K.A., Boyle, C., and Roffey, S. (2019) 'Creating a culture of belonging in a school context'. *Educational and Child Psychology* 36 (4), 5–7.

Allen, K.A., and Kern, M.L. (2017) *School Belonging in Adolescents: Theory, research, and practice*. Singapore: Springer.

Allen, K.A., and Kern, M.L. (2019) *Boosting School Belonging in Adolescents: Interventions for teachers and mental health professionals*. London: Routledge.

Allen, K.A., Kern, M.L., Vella-Brodrick, D., Hattie, J., and Waters, L. (2018) 'What schools need to know about belonging: A meta-analysis'. *Educational Psychology Review* 30 (1), 1–34. https://doi.org/10.1007/s10648-016-9389-8.

Allen, K. A., Vella-Brodrick, D., and Waters, L. (2017) 'School belonging and the role of social and emotional competencies in fostering an adolescent's sense of connectedness to their school'. In E. Frydenberg, A.J. Martin and R.J. Collie (eds), *Social and Emotional Learning in Australia and the Asia-Pacific: Perspectives, Programs and Approaches* (Singapore: Springer), pp. 83–99. https://doi.org/10.1007/978-981-10-3394-0_5.

Allen, T., Riley, K., and Coates, M. (2020) *Belonging, Behaviour and Inclusion in Schools: What does research tell us?* London: National Education Union. Available at: www.theartofpossiblities.org.uk/research.html. Accessed 23 November 2021.

American School Health Association (2009) 'Wingspread declaration on school connections'. *Journal of School Health* 74 (7), 233–4. doi: 10.1111/j.1746-1561 2004.tb08279.x.

Arslan, G., Allen, K., and Ryan, T. (2020) 'Exploring the impacts of school belonging on youth well-being and mental health: A longitudinal study'. *Child Indicators Research* 13, 1619–35. https://doi.org/10.1007/s12187-020-09721-z.

Auld, R. (1976) *William Tyndale, Junior and Infants School, Public Inquiry: A report to the Inner-London Education Authority by Robin Auld QC*. London: Inner London Education Authority.

Bailey, M., and West, S. (2020) 'Covid-19: Why compassionate leadership matters in a crisis'. https://www.kingsfund.org.uk/blog/2020/03/covid-19-crisis-compassionate-leadership. Accessed 25 October 2021.

Barnett, E. (2015) 'Stop pitying British schoolgirls joining Islamic State – they're not victims'. *Daily Telegraph*. http://www.telegraph.co.uk/women/wpomens-life/11429775/Schoolgirls-joining-Islamic-State-are-not-victims.-Stop-pitying-them.html. Accessed 25 February 2015.

Bauman, Z. (2006) *Liquid Fear*. Cambridge: Polity Press.

BBC News (2014) 'Margaret Thatcher's criticism of Brixton riot revealed'. 30 December 2014. https://www.bbc.co.uk/news/uk-30600064. Accessed 25 October 2021.

Berg, A.C., Melaville, A., and Blank, M.J. (2006) *Community and Family Engagement: Principals share what works*. Washington, DC: Coalition for Community Schools, Institute for Educational Leadership.

Big Issue (2017) 'Rise in hate crimes post Brexit'. *Big Issue*, 26 September–2 October.

Bloody Good Period and Women for Refugee Women (2019) 'The effects of "period poverty" among refugee and asylum-seeking women'. https://e13c0101-31be-4b7a-b23c-df71e9a4a7cb.filesusr.com/ugd/ae82b1_22dcc28fa137419abf5c9abe6bbf3b45.pdf. Accessed 25 October 2021.

Blum, R.W. (2005) 'A case for school connectedness'. *Adolescent Learner* 62 (7), 16–20. https://www.researchgate.net/publication/290823214. Accessed 23 November 2021.

Bourdieu, P. (1999) 'Site effects'. In P. Bourdieu., A. Accords and P. Ferguson (eds), *The Weight of the World: Social suffering in contemporary society* (Stanford, CA: Stanford University Press), pp. 123–9.

Bradbury, A., and Roberts-Holmes, G. (2017) 'Grouping in early years and key stage 1 – a necessary evil?' https://neu.org.uk/latest/NEU-ability-grouping-research. Accessed 25 October 2021.

Brunn, M., and Delaney-Barmann, G. (2001) 'Migrant children and language policies'. *Rural Educator* 22 (3), 8–16.

Bryk, A., and Schneider, A.S. (2015) *Trust in Schools: A core resource for improvement.* New York: Russell Sage Foundation.

Bryk, A.S., and Thum, Y.M. (1989). 'The effects of high school organization on dropping out: An exploratory investigation'. *American Education Research Journal* 26 (3), 353–83.

Campbell, D. (2016) 'NHS figures show "shocking" rise in self-harm among young people'. *Guardian*, 23 October. https://www.theguardian.com/society/2016/oct/23/nhs-figures-show-shocking-rise-self-harm-young-people. Accessed 25 October 2021.

Chaudhari, S. (2017) 'Educating Greater Manchester'. http://www.theboltonnews.co.uk/news/15492706.School__39_s_response_to_arena_attack_will_feature_in_new_Channel_4___39_Educating__39__series. Accessed 25 October 2021.

Children's Society (2017) *The Good Childhood Report*. https://www.basw.co.uk/system/files/resources/basw_53118-7_0.pdf. Accessed 6 December 2021.

Children's Society (2020a) 'Impact of Covid-19 on young people'. https://www.childrenssociety.org.uk/sites/default/files/2021-01/the-impact-of-covid-19-on-children-and-young-people-briefing.pdf. Accessed 6 December 2021.

Children's Society (2020b) 'Life on Hold: Children's well-being and COVID-19'. https://www.childrenssociety.org.uk/sites/default/files/2020-10/life-on-hold-childrens-well-being-and-covid-19.pdf. Accessed 6 December 2021.

Clarke, S., and Wildy, H. (2011) 'Providing professional sustenance for leaders of learning: The glass half-full?' In T. Townsend and J. MacBeath (eds), *International Handbook for Leadership in Learning* (Dordrecht: Springer), pp. 673–90.

Coard, B. (1971) *How the West Indian Child Is Made Educationally Sub-normal in the British School System: The scandal of the black child in schools in Britain*. London: New Beacon Books.

Coates, M. (2018) *It's Doing My Head In.* Melton: John Catt.

Coleman, J.S. (1988) 'Social capital in the creation of human capital'. *American Journal of Sociology* 94, S95–S120.

Connell, J.P., and Wellborn, J.G. (1991) 'Competence, autonomy and relatedness: A motivational analysis of self-system processes'. In M.R. Gunnar and L.A. Sroufe (eds), *Minnesota Symposium on Child Psychology* 22: 43–77. Hillsdale, NJ: Lawrence Erlbaum Associates.

Coughlan, S. (2017) 'Grammar school A-level row head suspended'. BBC News, 19 October. http://www.bbc.co.uk/news/education-41683012. Accessed 25 October 2021.

Coughlan, S. (2019) 'Pisa tests: UK rises in international school rankings'. BBC News, 3 December. https://www.bbc.com/news/education-50563833. Accessed 25 October 2021.

Creswell, T. (2004) *Place: A short introduction.* Oxford and Malden, MA: Blackwell.

Das Gupta, M. (2006) *Unruly Immigrants: Rights, activism, and transnational South East Asian politics in the United States*. Durham, NC: Duke University Press.

Demanet, J., and Van Houtte, M. (2012) 'School belonging and school misconduct: The differing role of teacher and peer attachment'. *Journal of Youth Adolescence* 41, 499–514. https://doi.org/10.1007/s10964-011-9674-2.

Department for Education (2019) *Timpson Review of School Exclusion.* London: Department for Education.

Drake, K. (2017) 'Competing proposes of education: The case of underschooled immigrant students'. *Journal of Educational Change* 18 (3), 311–27.

Drucker, P. (1994) 'The age of social transformation'. *Atlantic Monthly* 274, 53–80.

Duncan-Andrade, J. (2012) 'Growing Roses in Concrete'. https://vimeo.com/53863431. Accessed 25 October 2021.

Dunleavy, G. and Burke, J. (2019) 'Fostering a sense of belonging at an international school in France: An experimental study'. *Journal of Educational and Child Psychology* 36 (4), 34–45.
Dyson, A., and Gallannaugh, F. (2008) 'School-level actions to promote community cohesion: A scoping map'. Technical report in Research Evidence in Education Library. London: EPPI-Centre, Social Science Research Unit, Institute of Education, University of London.
Eade, J. (2000) *Placing London: From imperial capital to global city*. Oxford: Berghahn.
Elliot, K., Sammons, P., Robertson, P., Power, S., Campbell, C., and Whitty, G. (2002) 'Perceived impact over the first year of the pilot New Community School Programme'. *Scottish Educational Review* 34 (2), 138–50.
Ellis, T., McWhirter, J., McColgan, D., and Haddow, B. (1976) *William Tyndale: The Teachers' Story*. London: Writers and Readers Publishing Cooperative.
Elmeski, M. (2013) 'Principals as leaders of school and community revitalization: A phenomenological study of three urban schools in Morocco'. *International Journal of Leadership in Education: Theory and Practice.* DOI: 10.1080/13603124.2013.815803.
Fair Education Alliance (2017) 'Third state of the nation report card, 2016–2017'. http://www.faireducation.org.uk/report-card. Accessed 25 October 2021.
Flutter, J., and Rudduck, J. (2004) *Consulting Pupils: What's in it for schools?* London: Routledge.
Friel, B. (1990) *Dancing at Lughnasa*. London: Faber and Faber.
Friel, B. (2005) *Home Place*. London: Faber and Faber.
Gavrielides, T. (2020) *New Directions in Preventing Violent Youth Radicalisation: Comparative and summary findings from the Youth Empowerment and Innovation Project (YEIP).* https://www.iars.org.uk/online/youth-empowerment-and-innovation-project-yeip. Accessed 25 October 2021.
Gehlbach, H., Brinkworth, M.E., King, A.M., Hsu, L.M., McIntyre, J., and Rogers, T. (2016) 'Creating birds of similar feathers: Leveraging similarity to improve teacher–student relationships and academic achievement'. *Journal of Educational Psychology* 108 (3), 342–52.
Gentleman, A. (2017) 'Trafficked and enslaved: The teenagers tending UK cannabis farms'. *Guardian*, 25 March. www.theguardian.com/society/2017/mar/25/trafficked-enslaved-teenagers-tending-uk-cannabis-farms-vietnamese. Accessed 25 October 2021.
Gentleman, A. (2020) *The Windrush Betrayal: Exposing the hostile environment*. London: Guardian Faber.
Gentleman, A. (2021) 'Windrush victim wrongly threatened with forced return to Jamaica in final years, report finds'. Guardian, 8 June. https://www.innertemplelibrary.com/2021/06/windrush-victim-wrongly-threatened-with-forced-return-to-jamaica-in-final-years-report-finds-the-guardian. Accessed 23 November 2021.
Giddens, A. (1984) The Constitution of Society: Outline of the theory of structuration. Berkeley: University of California Press.
Gilbert, P. (2013) The Compassionate Mind. London: Robinson.
Gill, K., Quilter-Pinner, H., and Swift, D. (2017) *Making the Difference: Breaking the link between school exclusion and social exclusion*. London: Institute for Public Policy Research. https/:IPPR/making-the-difference-report-october-2017.pdf. Accessed 25 October 2021.
Gillen-O'Neel, C., and Fuligni, A.J. (2013) 'A longitudinal study of school belonging and academic motivation across high school'. *Child Development* 84 (2), 678–92. https://www.researchgate.net/publication/260162074. Accessed 25 October 2021.
Gladstone, R. (2021) 'Famine looms in Ethiopia's war-ravaged Tigray region, UN says'. *New York Times*, 26 May. www.nytimes.com/2021/05/26/world/africa/ethiopia-tigray-famine.html. Accessed 25 October 2021.
Glasman, N.S., and Crowson, R.L. (2001) 'Re-examining relations and a sense of place between schools and their constituents'. *Peabody Journal of Education* 76 (2), 1–8.
Goodenow, C. (1993) 'Classroom belonging among early adolescent students: Relationships to motivation and achievement'. *Journal of Early Adolescence* 13 (1) 21–4.
Goodenow, C., and Grady, K.E. (1993) 'The relationship of school belonging and friends' values to academic motivation among adolescent students'. *Journal of Experimental Education* 62 (1), 60–71. https://doi.org/10.1080/00220973.1993.9943831.
Gurr, D., Drysdale, L., Clarke, S., and Wildy, H. (2014) 'High-need schools in Australia: The leadership of two principals'. *Management in Education* 28 (3), 86–90.
Hague, C., and Jenkins, P. (2005) *Place Identity, Planning and Participation.* London and New York: Routledge.

Harari, Y.N. (2020) 'The world after coronavirus'. *Financial Times*, 20 March. https://www.ft.com/content/19d90308-6858-11ea-a3c9-1fe6fedcca75. Accessed 25 October 2021.

Helliwell, J.F., and Putnam, R.D. (2007) 'Education and social capital'. *Eastern Economic Journal* 33 (1), 1–19.

Henrich, C.C., Brookmeyer, K.A., and Shahar, G. (2005) 'Weapon violence in adolescence: Parent and school connectedness as protective factors'. *Journal of Adolescent Health* 37 (4), 306–12.

Hill, A., Mellon, L., Laker, B.B., and Goddard, J. (2017) 'Research: How the best school leaders create enduring change'. *Harvard Business Review*. https://hbr.org/2016/10/the-one-type-of-leader-who-can-turn-around-a-failing-school. Accessed 25 October 2021.

Hutchinson, J., and Crenna-Jennings, W. (2019) *Unexplained Pupil Exits from Schools: A growing problem?* Working paper. London: National Education Union and the Education Policy Institute.

IEA [International Association for the Evaluation of Educational Achievement] (2019) 'Do both boys and girls feel safe at school and does it matter?' *Compass Briefs in Education* 5. Amsterdam: IEA.

Ishimaru, A.M. (2018) 'Re-imagining turnaround: Families and communities leading educational justice'. *Journal of Educational Administration* 56 (5), 546–61. DOI 10.1108/JEA-01-2018-0013.

ITN (1981) TV Interview of Margaret Thatcher for ITN, 13 April. Transcript at https://www.margaretthatcher.org/document/104617. Accessed 25 October 2021.

Jaffer, N. (2015) 'The secret world of ISIS brides'. *Guardian*, 20 June. https://www.theguardian.com/world/2015/jun/24/isis-brides-secret-world-jihad-western-women-syria. Accessed 23 November 2021.

JCWI (2021) 'The hostile environment explained'. https://www.jcwi.org.uk/the-hostile-environment-explained. Accessed 25 October 2021.

John, G. (2011). *Mending Broken Britain? Education's response.* http://www.gusjohn.com/category/gus-talks/lectures/. Accessed 3 April 2019.

Johnson, M.K., Crosnoe, R., and Elder, G.H., Jr (2001) 'Students' attachment and academic engagement: The role of race and ethnicity'. *Sociology of Education* 74 (4), 318–40.

Kellet, M. (2010) *Rethinking Children and Research: Attitudes in contemporary society.* London: Bloomsbury.

Kernan, M. (2010) 'Space and place as a source of belonging and participation in urban environments: Considering the role of early childhood education and care settings'. *European Early Childhood Education Research Journal* 18 (2), 199–213. https://doi.org/10.1080/13502931003784420.

Kings Fund (2020) 'Covid 19: Why compassionate leadership matters in a crisis'. kingsfund.org.uk/blog/2020/03/covid-19-crisis-compassionate-leadership. Accessed 23 November 2021.

Koyama, J., and Rwehumbiza Bakuza, F. (2017) 'A timely opportunity for change: Increasing refuge parental involvement in US schools'. *Journal of Educational Change* 18 (3), 331–6.

Lacoe, J.R. (2015) 'Unequally safe: The race gap in school safety'. *Youth Violence and* Juvenile Justice 13 (2), 143–68.

Levin, B. (2000) 'Putting students at the centre in education reform'. *Journal of Educational Change* 1 (2), 155–72.

Lonczak, H.S., Abbott, R.D., Hawkins, J.D., Kosterman, R., and Catalano, R. (2002) 'The effects of the Seattle social development project: Behavior, pregnancy, birth, and sexually transmitted disease outcomes by age 21'. *Archives of Pediatric Adolescent Medicine* 156, 438–47.

Louis, K.S. (2007) 'Trust and improvement in schools'. *Journal of Educational Change* 8 (1), 1–25.

Louis, K.S., Smylie, M., and Murphy, J. (2016) 'Caring leadership for schools: Findings from exploratory analyses'. *Education Administration Quarterly* 52 (2), 310–48. https://doi.org/10.1177/0013161X15627678.

Lovett, S., Dempster, N., and Fluckiger, B. (2015). 'Personal agency in leadership learning using an Australian heuristic'. *Professional Development in Education* 41 (1), 127–43. https://doi.org/10.1080/19415257.2014.891532.

Ma, X. (2003) 'Sense of belonging to school: Can schools make a difference?' *Journal of Education Research* 96 (6), 340–9. http://dx.doi.org/10.1080/00220670309596617.

MacBeath, J., Myers, K., and Demitrou, H. (2001) 'Supporting teachers in consulting pupils about aspects of teaching and learning and evaluating impact'. *Forum* 43 (2), 78–82.

Martinez, S. P. (2018) 'Transforming the spaces into places'. In K. Riley., M. Coates, M. and S. P. Martinez, *Place and Belonging in Schools: Unlocking possibilities.* London: UCL Institute of

Education. https://www.ucl.ac.uk/ioe/sites/ioe/files/place-and-belonging-unlocking-possibilities.pdf. Accessed 25 October 2021.
Maslow, A. (1943) 'A theory of human motivation'. *Psychological Review* 50 (4), 370–96.
McMahon, S., Parnes, A., Keys, C., and Viola, J. (2008) 'School belonging among low-income urban youth with disabilities: Testing a theoretical model'. *Psychology in the Schools* 45 (5), 387–401.
Mehri, M. (2018) 'The ballad of the blade'. https://www.bbc.co.uk/programmes/b0bjzvd9. Accessed 25 October 2021.
Mitra, D. (2018) 'Student voice in secondary schools: The possibility for deeper change'. *Journal of Educational Administration* 56 (5), 473–87. DOI 10.1108/JEA-01-2018-0007.
Moody, J., and Bearman, P.S. (2004) 'Suicide and friendships among American adolescents'. *American Journal of Public Health* 94 (1), 89–95.
Morris, V., and Morris, C. (2002) 'Caring – the missing C in teacher education: Lessons learned from a segregated African American school'. *Journal of Teacher Education* 53 (2), 120–2.
Mortimore, P., Sammons, P., Stoll, L., and Lewis, D. (1988) *School Matters*. Berkeley: University of California Press.
Murphy, J.A., and Torre, D. (2015) *Understanding Schooling through the Eyes of Students*. Working paper. Nashville, TN: Vanderbilt University.
Murphy, L.T. (2017) 'Labor and sex trafficking among homeless youth'. https://oag.ca.gov/sites/all/files/agweb/pdfs/ht/murphy-labor-sex-trafficking-homeless-youth.pdf. Accessed 23 November 2021.
Myles, O., Boyle, C., and Richards, A. (2019) 'The social experiences and sense of belonging in adolescent females with autism in mainstream schools'. *Journal of Educational and Child Psychology* 36 (4), 8–21.
Naicker, I., Chikoko, V., and Mthiyane, S.E. (2014) 'Instructional leadership practices in challenging school contexts'. *Education as Change* 17, S137–S150.
O'Brien, K.A., and Bowles, T.V. (2013) 'The importance of belonging for adolescents in secondary school settings'. *European Journal of Social and Behavioural Sciences* 5(2), 976–84. http://dx.doi.org/10.15405/ejsbs.72.
OECD (2007). *Human Capital: How what you know shapes your life*. Paris: OECD.
OECD (2012) 'Programme for International Assessment (PISA) United Kingdom country note' – results from PISA 2012. Paris: OECD. www.oecd.org/pisa. Accessed 1 May 2018.
OECD (2013) 'PISA 2012 results in focus. What 15-year-olds know and what they can do with what they know'. Paris: OECD.
OECD (2017) *PISA 2015 Results*, volume 3, *Students' Well-Being*. Paris: OECD. https://dx.doi.org/10.1787/9789264273856-en. Accessed 25 October 2021.
OECD (2019) 'Sense of belonging at school'. *PISA 2018 Results*, volume 3, chapter 9. Paris: OECD. https://www.oecd-ilibrary.org/sites/d69dc209-en/index.html?itemId=/content/component/d69dc209-en. Accessed 25 October 2021.
OECD, (2020) *PISA 2018 Results*, volume 6, *Are Students Ready to Thrive in an Interconnected World?* Paris: OECD. https://www.oecd.org/publications/pisa-2018-results-volume-vi-d5f68679-en.htm. Accessed 25 October 2021.
ONS (2020) 'Online bullying in England and Wales: Year ending March 2020'. https://www.ons.gov.uk/peoplepopulationandcommunity/crimeandjustice/bulletins/onlinebullyinginenglandandwales/yearendingmarch2020. Accessed 25 October 2021.
Ofsted (2021) 'Review of sexual abuse in schools and colleges'. https://www.gov.uk/government/publications/review-of-sexual-abuse-in-schools-and-colleges/review-of-sexual-abuse-in-schools-and-colleges. Accessed 25 October 2021.
Osler, A. (2010) *Students' Perspectives on Schooling*. Maidenhead: Open University Press.
Pantic, N. (2015) 'A model for study of teacher agency for social justice'. *Teachers and Teaching; Theory and Practice* 21 (6), 759–78. doi: 10.1080/13540602.2015.104433.
Parr, E.J., Shochet, I.M., Cockshaw, W.D., and Kelly, R.L. (2020) 'General belonging is a key predictor of adolescent depressive symptoms and partially mediates school belonging'. *School Mental Health* 12 (3), 626–37. https://eric.ed.gov/?q=m&=a&pg=1157&id=EJ1263898.
Plan International (2017) UK research on period poverty and stigma. https://plan-uk.org/media-centre/plan-international-uks-research-on-period-poverty-and-stigma. Accessed 4 July 2021.
Pollard, A., Triggs, P., Broadbent, P., McNess, E., and Osborn, M. (2000) *What Pupils Say: Changing policy and practice in primary education*. London: Continuum.
Putnam. R.D. (2000) *Bowling Alone: The collapse and revival of American community*. New York: Simon and Schuster.

Putnam, R.D. (2015) *Our Kids: The American dream in crisis.* New York: Simon and Schuster.
Putnam, R.D., with Romney Garrett, S. (2020) *The Upswing: How we came together a century ago and how we can do it again*. Rugby: Swift Press.
Qureshi, A., Morris, M., and Mort, L. (2020) 'Access denied: The human impact of the hostile environment'. London: Institute for Public Policy Research. www.ippr.org/files/2020-09/access-denied-hostile-environment-sept20.pdf. Accessed 25 October 2021.
Ramphele, M. (1993) *A Bed Called Home: Life in the migrant labour hostels of Cape Town*. Cape Town: David Phillip.
Rampton Report (1981) *West Indian Children in our Schools*. Interim report of the Committee of Inquiry into the Education of Children from Ethnic Minority Groups. London: HMSO.
Rethinking Schools (2017). 'Little kids, big ideas, teaching social issues and global conflicts with young children'. *Rethinking Schools* 31 (4), 4–5.
Richardson, M. (2015) 'Agentic action in context'. In R. Young., J. Domene, and L. Valach (eds), *Counseling and Action* (New York: Springer), pp. 51–68.
Riley, K. (1982) 'Policing the police, teaching the teachers: Scarman, Rampton and MPs read the riot lessons'. *Multiracial Education* 10 (2), 63–76.
Riley, K. (1985a) *Attitudes and Aspirations of Girls of Afro Caribbean Origin*. Unpublished PhD thesis, Bulmershe College of Education/University of London/University of Cambridge.
Riley, K. (1985b) 'Black girls speak for themselves'. In G. Weiner (ed.), *Just a Bunch of Girls*. Milton Keynes: Open University Press.
Riley, K. (1994) *Quality and Equality: Promoting opportunities in schools.* London: Cassell.
Riley, K. (1998) *Whose School is it Anyway?* London: Falmer Press.
Riley, K. (2007) *Surviving and Thriving as an Urban Leader: Reflective and analytical tools for leaders of our city schools.* London: Institute of Education/Esmée Fairbairn Foundation.
Riley, K. (2008) 'Improving city schools: Who and what makes the difference?' In C. Sugre (ed.), *New Directions for Educational Change: International perspectives* (London: Routledge), pp. 155–71.
Riley, K. (2013a) *Leadership of Place: Stories from schools in the US, UK and South Africa*. London: Bloomsbury.
Riley, K. (2013b) 'Walking the leadership tightrope: Building community cohesiveness and social capital in schools in highly disadvantaged urban communities'. *British Educational Research Journal* 39 (2), 266–86.
Riley, K. (2017) *Place, Belonging and School Leadership: Researching to make the difference*. London: Bloomsbury.
Riley, K. (2019a) 'We're a long way from a sense of belonging'. *Times Educational Supplement*, 7 June, 21–2.
Riley, K. (2019b) 'Agency and belonging: What transformative actions can schools take to help create a sense of place and belonging?' *Journal of Educational and Child Psychology* 36 (4), 91–103.
Riley, K., Coates, M., and Allen, T. (2020) *Place and Belonging in School: Why it matters today*. London: National Education Union. https://neu.org.uk/media/13026/view. Accessed 25 October 2021.
Riley, K., Coates, M., and Perez Martinez, S. (2018) *Place and Belonging in Schools: Unlocking possibilities.* London: UCL Institute of Education. https://www.ucl.ac.uk/ioe/sites/ioe/files/place-and-belonging-unlocking-possibilities.pdf. Accessed 25 October 2021.
Riley, K., and Docking, J. (2004) 'Voices of disaffected pupils: Implications for policy and practice'. *British Journal of Educational Studies* 52(2), 166–79. https://doi.org/10.1111/j.1467-8527.2004.00261.x.
Riley, K., Ellis, S., Weinstock, W., Tarrant, J., and Hallman, S. (2006) 'Re-engaging disaffected pupils in learning: Insights for policy and practice'. *Improving Schools* 9 (1), 17–31.
Riley, K., and Emery, H. (2007) 'Reconfiguring urban school leadership: Some lessons from London'. In T. Brighouse and L. Fullich (eds), *Education in a Global City: Essays from London* (London: Institute of Education), pp. 169–96.
Riley, K., and MacBeath, J. (1998) 'Effective leaders and effective schools'. In J. MacBeath (ed.), *Effective School Leadership: Responding to change*. London: Paul Chapman.
Riley, K., and Mendoza, M. (2020) *Leading in a New Era: Compassionate leadership for place and belonging, a research inquiry*. https://education.hackney.gov.uk/sites/default/files/document/Leading%20in%20a%20New%20Era.pdf. Accessed 25 October 2021.

Riley, K., Mendoza, M., and Gonzales, S. (2020) *Cross-Sector and Interdisciplinary Perspectives on School Belonging and Exclusion: What we know; what we need to know; and what needs to change.* London: UCL Institute of Education.

Riley, K., Montecinos, C., and Ahumada, L. (2016) 'Effective principals serving in high poverty schools in Chile: Managing competing realities'. *Procedia – Social and Behavioral Sciences* 237, 843–9. http://dx.doi.org/10.1016/j.sbspro.2017.02.181.

Riley, K., and Rustique-Forrester, E. (2002) *Why Children Lose Interest in School and What We Can Do About It*. London: Chapman Sage.

Roffey, S., and Boyle, C. (2018) 'Belief, belonging and the role of schools in reducing the risk of home-grown extremism', In K.A. Allen and C. Boyle (eds), *Pathways to Belonging: Contemporary research in school belonging*. Leiden: Brill.

Rustin, A. (2017) 'Grenfell: six months on'. *Guardian*, 14 December 2017, 7.

Rutter, M., Maugham, B., Mortimer, P., and Ouston, J., with Smith, A. (1979). *Fifteen Thousand Hours: Secondary schools and their effects on children*. London: Harvard University Press.

Samdal, O., Nutbeam, D., Wold, B., and Kannas, L. (1998) 'Achieving health and educational goals through schools: A study of the importance of the climate and students' satisfaction with school'. *Health Education Research* 3, 383–97.

Sánchez, B., Colón, Y., and Esparza, P. (2005) 'The role of sense of school belonging and gender in the academic adjustment of Latino adolescents'. *Journal of Youth and Adolescence* 34 (6), 619–28. doi: https://doi.org/10.1007/s10964-005-8950-4.

Savage, M. (2020) 'Drug gangs prey on excluded truants'. *Guardian*, 29 November, 21. Scarman Inquiry (1981) *Inquiry into the 1981 Brixton Disturbances*. London: HMSO.

Schleicher, A. (2019) 'PISA 2018: Insights and interpretations'. https://www.oecd.org/pisa/PISA%202018%20Insights%20and%20Interpretations%20FINAL%20PDF.pdf. Accessed 25 October 2021.

Seashore, K.L., and Murphy, J.F. (2018) 'The Potential of positive leadership for school improvement: A cross-disciplinary synthesis'. *Nordic Journal of Comparative and International Education* 2, 2–3.

Sellgren, K., and Wills, E. (2021) 'Girls asked for nudes by up to 11 boys a night, Ofsted finds'. BBC News, 10 June. https://www.bbc.co.uk/news/education-57411363?xtor=ES-208-[44752_NEWS_NLB_ACT_WK24_Thurs_10_June]-20210611. Accessed 25 October 2021.

Sergiovanni, T.J. (1992) *Moral Leadership: Getting to the heart of school improvement.* San Francisco: Jossey-Bass.

Shochet, I.M., Smyth, T.L., and Homel, R. (2007) 'The impact of parental attachment on adolescent perception of the school environment and school connectedness'. *Australian and New Zealand Journal of Family Therapy* 28 (2), 109–18.

Sinek, S. (2009) *Start With Why: How great leaders inspire everyone to take action*. London: Portfolio Penguin.

Sirin, S.R., and Rogers-Sirin, L. (2004). 'Exploring school engagement of middle-class African American adolescents'. *Youth and Society* 35 (3), 323–40.

Smylie, M.A., Murphy, J., and Seashore Louis, K. (2020) *The Practice of Caring School Leadership*. Thousand Oaks, CA: Corwin Press.

Steiner, R.J., Sheremenko, G., Lesesne, C., Dittus, P.J., Sieving, R.E., and Ethier, K.A. (2019) 'Adolescent connectedness and adult health outcomes'. *Pediatrics* 144 (1), e20183766.

Taylor, M. (2020) *Creating Change for the 'Pinball' Kid*. London: RSA.

Teach First (2019) 'GCSE subjects reveal stark unfairness faced by disadvantaged pupils'. https://www.teachfirst.org.uk/press-release/New-investigation-into-GCSE-subjects-reveals-the-stark-extent-that-disadvantaged-pupils-are-being-left-behind. Accessed 25 October 2021.

Telford and Wrekin Council (2019) *Belonging Strategy*. https://www.annafreud.org/media/12700/telford-and-wrekin-belonging-strategy-brochure.pdf. Accessed 25 October 2021.

Turner, C. (2021) 'Watchdog to inspect private schools caught up in "rape culture" scandal'. *Daily Telegraph*, 7 April. Telegraph.co.uk/news/2021/04/07/watchdog-inspect-private-schools-caught-rape-culture-scandal. Accessed 23 November 2021.

Tyrell, I., and Griffin, J. (2013). *The Human Givens: A new approach to emotional health and clear thinking*. Chalvington: Human Givens Publishing.

UNHCR (2015) 'Figures at a glance'. http://www.unhcr.org/pages/49c3646c11.html. Accessed 25 October 2021.

UNHCR (2021) ‘UNHCR warns of mounting refugee and migrant deaths in the Central Mediterranean’. https://www.unhcr.org/news/briefing/2021/5/609134f74/unhcr-warns-mounting-refugee-migrant-deaths-central-medite. Accessed 25 October 2021.

UNICEF (2017) ‘Humanitarian action for children 2017: Overview’. https://www.unicef.org/media/49726/file/HAC_2017_Overview_ENG.pdf. Accessed 23 November 2021.

Van Ryzin, M.J., Gravely, A.A., and Roseth, C.J. (2009) ‘Autonomy, belongingness, and engagement in school as contributors to adolescent psychological well-being’. *Journal of Youth and Adolescence* 38 (1), 1–12.

Weale, S., and Fishwick, C. (2017) ‘Schools around England ejecting “underperforming” sixth-formers’. *Guardian*, 30 August. https://www.theguardian.com/education/2017/aug/30/mps-attack-ejection-of-underperforming-sixth-formers. Accessed 25 October 2021.

Weil, S. (2002 [1952]) *The Need for Roots: Prelude to a declaration of duties towards mankind.* London: Routledge Classics.

West-Burnham, J. (2015) *Moral Leadership.* https://www.unrwa.org/userfiles/file/leading_4_the_future/module1/moral-leadership%20West%20Burnham.pdf. Accessed 25 October 2021.

Wike, T.L., and Fraser, M.W. (2009) ‘School shootings: Making sense of the senseless’. *Aggression and Violent Behavior* 14 (3), 162–9.

Williams, K.D., Forgas, J.P., and von Hippel, W. (2005) *The Social Outcast: Ostracism, social exclusion, rejection, and bullying*. Cambridge: Cambridge University Press.

Willms, J.D. (2003) *Student engagement at school, a sense of belonging and participation: Results from Pisa 2000*. Paris: OECD.

Wilson, D., and Elliott, D. (2003) ‘The interface of school climate and school connectedness: an exploratory review and study’. Paper presented at the Wingspread Conference on School Connectedness, Racine, WI.

Wyman, P.A., Pickering, T.A., Pisani, A.R., Rulison, K., Schmeelk-Cone, K., Hartley, C., Gould, M., Caine, E.D., LoMurray, M., Brown, C.H., and Valente, T.W. (2019) ‘Peer-adult network structure and suicide attempts in 38 high schools: implications for network-informed suicide prevention’. *Journal of Child Psychology and Psychiatry* 60 (10), 1065–75.

Zephaniah, B. (2016) ‘We refugees’. In *Wicked World.* London: Penguin.

Zimmer-Gembeck, M.J., Chipuer, H.M., Hanisch, M., Creed, P.A., and McGregor, L. (2006) ‘Relationships at school and stage-environment fit as resources for adolescent engagement and achievement’. *Journal of Adolescence* 29 (6), 911–33.

Index

Italic page numbers indicate figures.

www.ingramcontent.com/pod-product-compliance
Lightning Source LLC
LaVergne TN
LVHW052018300826
846742LV00020B/87